The
AMERICAN PARTY BATTLE

THE MACMILLAN COMPANY
NEW YORK · BOSTON · CHICAGO · DALLAS
ATLANTA · SAN FRANCISCO

MACMILLAN & CO., Limited
LONDON · BOMBAY · CALCUTTA
MELBOURNE

THE MACMILLAN CO. OF CANADA, Ltd.
TORONTO

THE · WORLD · TODAY · BOOKSHELF

The American Party Battle

By CHARLES A. BEARD ~ ~ ~ ~

Joint Author of
"The Rise of American Civilization"

Published by THE MACMILLAN COMPANY
at Sixty Fifth Avenue, New York
City ~ ~ ~ ~ ~ ~ 1928

PREFACE

This is an attempt to present within the compass of a small volume a general sketch of American party history. Of course, there are dangers in such over-simplification, in making bold strokes which do not record fine shades and distinctions. Yet there are advantages, too, in an effort to see the party battle in its broad outlines, with the permanent and continuous essentials emphasized.

In preparing this book I have drawn upon my larger work, *American Government and Politics.* Other borrowings have been made from *The Rise of American Civilization.* These materials, however, have been recast.

Charles A. Beard.

New Milford, Conn.,
August, 1928.

CONTENTS

vii

CONTENTS—Continued

The
AMERICAN PARTY BATTLE

THE AMERICAN PARTY BATTLE

CHAPTER I

NATURE OF POLITICAL PARTIES

§ *Origin of Parties*

WHY do political parties arise? The question is hard to answer. Certainly the solutions of the problem offered by writers on the subject are vague and contradictory.

According to one view, politics is merely a great game or sport, an endless contest between the ins and outs, full of sound and fury, springing from no substantial interests, affecting in no vital way the state of the people. Citizens divide into political parties for reasons no more important than those which separate them into partisans of Gene Tunney or Jack Dempsey. Politics is all a question of finding slogans that will capture the crowd or discovering candidates that will awaken enthusiasm. "If the Republicans can find the proper candidate," remarks Dr. George B. Cutten, President of Colgate University, in the Sunday Times of May 13, 1928, "almost any kind of a slogan will do; if the Democrats can find the proper slogan almost any kind of a candidate will do."

Another explanation of party origins is to be found in the writings of the English historian, Lord Macaulay. According to his interpretation, men (and presumably women) divide *naturally* into two groups—one devoted to order, conservative in disposition, and the other devoted to progress, adventurous in character. In short, the problem is one of psychology.

A similar answer to the riddle was made a few years ago by a distinguished professor of literature, Brander Matthews. Americans, he declared, divide *instinctively* into Hamiltonians and Jeffersonians. "The Hamiltonian," he said, "believes in government by the best, by the selected leaders, competent to guide the less competent mass; and this is true aristocracy in the best sense of that abused word. The Jeffersonian believes that the average man, however unenlightened, actually knows his own business, or at least knows what he wants, better than any superior person can know it for him; and this is true democracy in the best sense of that abused term. These two attitudes are inevitably antagonistic; they are instinctive, intuitive, innate."[1]

Of course this is like saying, "God made Democrats and Republicans, and that is all there is to it." When anyone states that human actions spring from innate, inherent, intuitive sources, he denies the force of environment and with a final air disposes of such little questions as: "Why are they innate? How do you know that they are innate? Where is the proof?"

Furthermore a detailed study of political parties, always disconcerting to the makers of simple hypotheses, reveals some data not easily disposed of by the literary theory of politics. Parties in Europe do not divide into two sections: conservative and progressive, Hamiltonian and Jeffersonian. There we find labor parties, agrarian parties, clerical parties, industrialist parties, Hungarian, German, Polish, and what-not parties. A study of the early distribution of party membership in the United States shows that the major portion of the Hamiltonian party had its center of influence in the cities and towns where financial, industrial, and commercial interests were predominant. Hamilton was a New York lawyer. Leadership

---

1. New York Times Magazine, September 24, 1916.

THE AMERICAN PARTY BATTLE

in the Jeffersonian party came from the slave-owning planters of the South. Jefferson was a Southern planter.

How did it happen that most of the business men of the country were instinctive Hamiltonians, intuitive "aristocrats," and most of the aristocratic planters of the South became instinctive Jeffersonians, intuitive "democrats?" The matter is not as simple as Mr. Matthews imagined.

On about the same footing may be placed the explanation of party divisions offered by James Bryce in his great work, *The American Commonwealth*. According to his view, the history of American parties began about 1787 when two opposing tendencies were "revealed"—one in favor of strengthening the central government and the other in favor of upholding the "sovereign" rights of the states. Broadly speaking, one party has advocated an extensive use of federal powers and the other has opposed that operation. Perhaps this may be called the orthodox theory of American party differences.

To this interpretation two objections can be made. The first is that neither party has been consistent in upholding its creed — particularly whenever its vital interests have been affected. For example, the Jeffersonians used federal powers to the limit in purchasing Louisiana, in putting an embargo on commerce, and in enacting the fugitive slave law of 1850 for the return of runaway property. On the other hand, the Hamiltonians, who stretched federal powers in establishing a bank and making protective tariffs, became advocates of state's rights when they opposed the purchase of Louisiana and resisted the enforcement of the embargo.[1]

The second objection to the Bryce theory is that it explains nothing. Why did some of the American people think that the federal government should be strong and others give their affection to the states—that is, when upon occasion it suited their pleasure to do so? Did this division have a direct relation to the occupations and interests of the people? Was it not geared up to pre-existing differences in work and economy? As the theory stands, it merely offers another illusive "innate" clue to the origin of parties.

More realistic and therefore more illuminating is the key to party differences given in the tenth number of the Federalist by James Madison, the "Father of the federal Constitution" and twice

---

1. See below, pp. 53-54.

President of the United States. "The most common and durable source of factions [that is, in eighteenth century language, parties]," Madison said, "has been the various and unequal distribution of property. Those who hold and those who are without property have ever formed distinct interests in society. Those who are creditors and those who are debtors fall under a like distinction. A landed interest, a manufacturing interest, a mercantile interest, with many lesser interests grow up of necessity in civilized nations and divide them into different classes actuated by different sentiments and views. The regulation of these various and interfering interests forms the principal task of modern legislation and involves the spirit of party and faction in the necessary and ordinary operations of government."

In other words, the division of voters into parties according to their political sentiments and views springs from the possession of different kinds and amounts of property. Illustrations of this theory may be readily recalled by those familiar with the role of the farmer vote, the labor vote, and the business vote in American politics.

Though realistic, this theory must not be taken too narrowly. We are in great danger of being misled by such words as capitalists, farmers, and laborers. Capitalists, that is, people engaged in using money to make money, are certainly not all occupied in identical processes. Some are manufacturers of commodities which come into sharp competition with European products and favor high protective tariffs on their particular goods. Others are engaged in producing commodities not subject to competition and may be stanch free traders.

Again, capitalists interested in railways may be utterly indifferent to protective tariffs because it matters little to them whether they haul domestic or foreign freight.

A third group of capitalists are merchants who import many of the commodities they offer for sale and may look with pleasure upon low tariffs promising cheaper prices and larger turnovers.

Finally, there are the financiers, the bankers, who lend money to industries and governments, foreign and domestic, apparently without patriotic preference, considering the terms and security of their loans more important than national advantages. They may be indifferent as to the schedules in tariff bills; or they may approve low rates on imports which facilitate the payment of

[7]

interest and charges on loans floated abroad. Indeed there is apparent now a rift between the bankers and manufacturers of the United States with respect to tariff policies.

Hence we may conclude that bankers, railway investors, and importing merchants, all capitalists, might readily line up with Democratic cotton growers of the South in support of a low tariff campaign, assuming that the latter did not propose other radical measures calculated to alarm their allies.

Nor is the case much different with regard to the "agricultural interest." It too is divided into special interests. The cotton growers of the South produce a staple which is sold largely in foreign markets and they are subjected to little competition as yet from cotton raisers in other countries. Consequently they need no protection on their commodity and naturally favor a low tariff on the manufactured goods which they consume. On the other hand the raisers of wheat, corn, live-stock, and fruits have many formidable competitors and are generally found in the protective tariff lobbies when their particular commodities are under consideration. All this is made so clear by A. N. Holcombe in his book on *The*

Political Parties of To-day that comment is superfluous. One of the difficult tasks of political managers is to work out the proper combination that will unite the major portion of the farmers under one political roof.

Not a whit more solid is the much vaunted "solidarity of labor." Busily concerned with the question of wages, trade unionists cannot be entirely oblivious to the conditions which determine wages. Those who labor in mills heavily protected against foreign competition may easily allow their practical interests (supposed at least) to outweigh their opposition to capitalists and vote with their employers. Again, one industry may be very prosperous while others are in a state of depression. Miners may be starving while railway conductors and engineers are living well and making large deposits in their union banks.

It is also necessary to emphasize the "various and unequal distribution of property" mentioned by Madison. There are big and little capitalists, big and little farmers. Some are prosperous for one reason or another. Others are struggling along near the margin of subsistence or are heavily in debt. Hence the capitalistic and agricultural interests are criss-crossed by intricate lines due to "the various and unequal distribution of property." It takes a great deal of research and discernment to find the roots of "different sentiments and views" in any particular political situation, especially as it is hard to get all the pertinent data in the case.

Additional difficulties in applying Madison's theory arise from the fact that two persons in the same economic situation and cherishing the same "sentiments" may differ as to the best plan of action to advance their interests. Their motive may be purely economic and their prejudices identical, but their reasoning divergent. For example, two capitalists confronted by a menacing labor agitation may utterly disagree as to the best method for dealing with it. One may favor calling in the police and the other urge the expediency of conciliatory tactics.

Presumably most of the directing classes know what their interests are, at least in detail; but they often make wrong guesses as to policies calculated to bring advantages to them in the long run. Moreover, as society becomes more complicated, the difficulties of figuring up the exact results likely to flow from particular types of action increase. It is at this point that intelligence and information enter into policy-determining operations. If two people of the same economic class, seeking the same economic advantage, disagree on methods, evidently in this case the theory of economic interpretation breaks down; that is, it does not explain the divergence in political view. Even the dictatorship of the proletariat in Russia is marked by bitter dissensions over policy. Still, though it does not by any means exhaust the science of the subject, economics is a fundamental branch of politics and offers the most satisfactory clue to the origin and development of political parties.

Economics also runs into political situations which wear racial aspects. It is a matter of common observation, for example, that Irish-Americans are generally Democrats. A great deal of light can be thrown on this fact by economic history. In the beginning, the Irish who migrated to America were extremely poor in this world's goods and settled in the cities as laborers. For a generation or two most of them were hewers of wood and drawers of water—until other races from southern and southeastern Europe came to take their places and enabled them to move up in the industrial scale. As laborers, the Irish were generally drawn into the party of the masses and lined up against the classes. On the other hand, when the German migration set in heavily the federal government was giving away land in the West and thousands of Germans owed their farms to the bounty of the Republicans. This debt they did not forget.

To some degree religious sentiments are connected with economic situations. Catholic writers are fond of saying that the Protestant revolt against the Roman Church sprang from a lust of the rising middle class for the property of the clergy. Undoubtedly this was a factor in a momentous religious change. Its importance is now demonstrated in many scientific works. To use another illustration, the prevalence of Democratic party views among Catholics may be, to a considerable extent, attributed to the fact that a large proportion of the Catholics are of immigrant stock and are to be found in or close to the laboring ranks of American industrial society.

It is almost safe to say that, where diverse economic interests divide groups, common religious sentiments will not completely weld them. In other words, religious ties are not often strong enough to bind opposing economic interests into the same party. Protestant churches were divided in America over slavery, the Southern branches sustaining their "peculiar institution." Methodists and Baptists split over tariff schedules, the regulation of railway rates, farm relief, and other economic questions.

Confusion with respect to the roots of party differences is darkened by the very nature of party organization. It often happens that an institution, established for a clear and definite object, continues after its end has been attained. Herbert Spencer tells an amusing story of a society founded in England for the purpose of carrying on an agitation for a particular reform. It had its president, secretaries, agents, paid workers, and petty officers. After a long season of agitation, Parliament finally adopted the reform. Shortly after the triumph, Spencer called at the organization headquarters expecting to find great rejoicing. Instead he found universal sorrow. The achievement of the purposes of the society had abolished all the lucrative jobs which it maintained. So in politics.

A political party has offices and positions yielding gains and profits. When in possession of the government it distributes honors, privileges, favors, and emoluments of one kind or another. The spoils of office alone are sufficient to sustain a large party. Once in power and enjoying its advantages, professional politicians are loath to lose what they have gained. Out of power, they hesitate to espouse any ideas that will defeat their efforts to capture the government. Hence on both sides regular party workers often prefer to avoid rather than to define issues, especially when there is risk in definition. The significance of this operating cause in politics calls for a special examination into the nature of parties as organizations.

§ *The Nature of the Political Party*

It is customary to regard the party as composed of all those who vote its ticket, but this is a very loose idea. Thousands who vote with a party are independents or members of opposing parties, who for the time being favor its candidates and platforms. Additional thousands who regularly vote a ticket devote no thought or time to party debates and conferences, and could not give a fifty-word account of why they happen to be in that particular party. According to another definition, the term "party" covers just those who are openly enrolled on the party roster, as required by law or practice, and thus entitled to participate in party primaries. This group in fact consists of from thirty to eighty per cent of the party voters. The number who actually go to the primaries and take a hand in electing party officers and nominating candidates is still smaller than the party membership, ranging sometimes as low as ten per cent of the enrolled voters and not often higher than seventy per cent.

Among the fifty per cent who may be reckoned as taking some positive interest in the affairs of the party, only a small portion can be regarded as active and influential. There are at the center some loyal and zealous party members who believe that the welfare and safety of the Republic depend upon the principles which they advocate —members who hold no office and may be disinterested. But we have no political micrometer for measuring the size of this element in each party.

More constantly active, as a rule, are the regular and permanent officials of the party, such as the committee members and chairmen (national, state, and local), paid workers, office-holders dependent for their positions upon the party, would-be office-holders looking to the party for preferment, editors of party newspapers and representatives of various interests (real estate, commercial, industrial, labor, etc.), which expect favors at the hands of the party.

Once established, the party institution becomes a kind of *imperium in imperio*—a state within the state. It has its constitution, its officers, its laws, its treasury, its loyal subjects, and its penalties for treason. No one can hope to rise in politics except through the agency of some party. An independent citizen who refuses to call himself a party member is looked upon as a "crank" or a "goody-goody." A person who leaves his party and joins another is treated with contempt and scorn by his former colleagues. The vilest words in our political vocabulary are reserved for the party "deserter."

The whole spirit of party was accurately reflected long ago in the Richmond Whig's editorial on the "no-party man." "We heartily join in desiring the extermination of this pestiferous and demoralizing brood, and will do whatever we can to effect it. . . . Let the Whigs and Democrats everywhere resolve that the gentry who are too pure to associate with either of them or to belong to either party, shall not use them to their own individual aggrandizement. Let them act upon the principle that the Whig or Democrat who has sense enough to form an opinion and honesty enough to avow it is to be preferred to the imbecile or the purist or the mercenary, who cannot come to a decision, or is ashamed of his principles, or from sordid considerations is afraid to declare them."

The party alignment, sharp enough before the Civil War, became even sharper for a long time after that great crisis, so that political independence or sympathy with any "third party" principles came to be regarded as a species of treason coupled with intellectual dishonesty. "The party," says Ostrogorski, "became a sort of church which admitted no dissent and pitilessly excommunicated any one who deviated a hair's-breadth from the established dogma or ritual, were it even from a feeling of deep piety, from a yearning for a more perfect realization of the ideal of holiness set before the believer."

§ *The Roots and Sources of Party Strength*

Why is it that party organization has become so minute in its ramifications and so powerful in the United States? To answer that question adequately, one would have to explore the structure of American society; but some of the more obvious reasons are agreed upon and may be enumerated here.

In the first place, the large number of elective offices makes it impossible for the mass of the people to take an active part in nominating candidates and running the political machinery. Wherever elective officers are provided for, machinery for making nominations inevitably follows, with its long train of primaries, caucuses, conventions and committees. Each new elective office adds to the weight, strength, complexity, and immobility of the machine. Party business of necessity falls into the hands of professional workers experienced in the art of managing primaries and elections.

Even the very structure of our federal system makes party government and strong party organization indispensable if the will of the voters is to be realized. The legislative powers are divided between Congress and the states, so that if a party has a policy which requires federal and state action it must be in power in both governments. For example, if a party wants an interstate commerce law, it must go to Washington; if it wants a sup-

plementary law regulating commerce within the
state in a manner consistent with the federal law,
it must go to the state legislature. If a party,
therefore, has a systematic and national policy cov-
ering the important questions of our day relative
to railways, insurance, conservation, prohibition,
and trust regulation, it must embrace within its
plans federal and state laws; and in order to realize completely its program, it should be strong
enough to control state and national legislatures.

The legal separation of executive and legislative powers serves to strengthen the political party;
for democracy or majority rule, as now understood, requires the coordination of those two
branches of government, and the political party is
employed to bring them into harmony with each
other. To take a homely example from daily life:
no business man who has made up his mind that
a certain thing shall be done would think for a
moment of choosing an executive agent bitterly opposed to the plan. And yet this is exactly what may
happen and does often happen in American politics. It frequently occurs that the legislature of
a state is Republican and the governor Democratic; that is, legislators are chosen to make laws
which are to be enforced by an executive whose

party may be in violent opposition to those very laws.

In order, therefore, for popular government actually to function, it is necessary that those who have decided upon a certain public policy should control not only the makers of the law, but also the principal officials charged with its execution. In England, this fact is frankly recognized in the unwritten constitution; for the executive branch, that is, the Cabinet composed of the heads of departments, is usually selected from the party having a majority in the House of Commons. The makers of the law and those charged with its execution are one. In the United States, however, this coordination of the legislature and the executive must be secured *outside* the written law; and it is the party system which makes it possible. It is the party that assures the nomination of candidates who are in a fair degree of harmony with one another, and who, if elected, can work consistently together in legislative and executive positions to carry out the will of the voters expressed at the ballot box.

Passing outward from the structure of government, which in itself makes for strong party organization, we encounter the "spoils system" as a contributing factor. To some extent, of course, civil service reform has reduced the relative number of offices to be filled by party adherents, but there still remains an enormous number of federal and state positions to be divided among the victors. The political appointments subject to the President's orders have an annual value of millions. The multiplication of the functions of state administration has enlarged the appointing power of the governor and the state senate. Every state legislature has within its gift legislative offices and positions available for partisan purposes, usually free from civil service control. For example, there are sergeants-at-arms and assistant sergeants-at-arms, principal doorkeepers, first and second assistant doorkeepers, journal clerks, executive clerks, index clerks, revision clerks, librarians, messengers, postmasters, janitors, stenographers, and messengers to the various committees and assistants first and second, too numerous to mention. Then there are city offices, high and low, steadily multiplying in number, and, in spite of the civil service restrictions, within the gift of the political party that wins at the polls. Finally there are the election officers, a veritable army of inspectors, ballot clerks, and poll clerks for the primary and regular elections, who derive anywhere from $10 to $50 a year for their services. Every large city annually pays thousands of dollars to the officials who preside at primaries and elections.

Party machines are strengthened by huge levies on the candidates. Generally speaking, no one can hope to be elected to office to-day without being nominated by one of the political parties. The party organization wages the campaign which carries the candidate into office. What is more natural and just than the demand that the candidate shall help to pay the legitimate expenses of the campaign? It is a regular practice, therefore, for party organizations, state and local, to collect tribute from candidates for nomination as well as nominees to office—as a rule in proportion to the value of the office they seek. There are in addition levies on office-holders after election, sometimes in spite of the laws forbidding it. Office-holders do not always wait to be pressed by party managers in this matter. It is not expedient.

The construction of parks, school buildings, highways and other public works yields revenues to the party organization which controls the letting of contracts. High bids may be accepted on the condition that the surplus shall go to the party

war chest or to the party leaders. The capitol
building and grounds at Albany cost New York
nearly $25,000,000, and the plunder of the public
treasury in the construction of the capitol at Har-
risburg is a notorious chapter in Pennsylvania history.

Even more important, as an economic factor,
than the spoils of office are the large funds secured by party organizations from private interests and distributed by their officers and workers.[1] Perhaps the most fruitful source of revenue
for party treasuries during recent years has been
contributions from business corporations—even
though prohibited by law in many states. They
must all apply to the government, national, state
or municipal, for the right to come into existence
in the first place, and for the right to extend their
operations in the second place. They are subject
to constant regulation by municipal councils, state
legislatures, or Congress (possibly by all three
agencies) ; they are compelled to do things which
cost them large sums of money or to abstain from
doing things which are highly profitable. In these
circumstances, corporations often find it cheap to

---

1. J. K. Pollock, **Party Campaign Funds.**

pay party "bosses" for favors and immunities. With a kindred concern for practical ends, industrial concerns which thrive under protective tariffs often "insure themselves against free trade" by contributing generously to party war chests. Far more elusive is the collection of party revenues in return for the protection of gambling, liquor selling, and vice in various forms. The extent to which this source of funds is exploited at any time by any party is, of course, impossible to ascertain; but authentic documents show that in the not distant past huge sums for party war chests have come from the government protection of those who violate its laws.

Sometimes the private interests affected by governmental action give money to parties to secure favors or prevent regulations really designed in the public interest. Sometimes they are forced to contribute, "blackmailed", by party leaders under threats of punitive legislation if they do not. On many occasions, they have given money to both the leading parties with a view to getting a "friend at court" without fail.

Leaving the economic realm for that of social psychology, we are on a less secure ground in searching for the sources of party power, but here too are factors which contribute to the strength of political organizations. From the days of de Tocqueville to those of Bryce, foreign observers have noted that the people of America are given to the formation of associations of every kind. There are in the United States literally thousands of lodges, orders, and fraternal societies; there are political, social, benevolent, religious, and reform societies without number. It is a rare American who is not a member of five or six.

The causes of this zeal for association are obscure, but it may be in part attributed to the ferment of opinions in a democracy. Anyone who gets a new idea or a variant on an old one wants to start a society to propagate it. There are practical benefits, too, which are not to be ignored— assistance in business, trade, and professions. The phenomenon has also been attributed by some acute foreign observers to the weakness of the individual and the power of the mass where theories of equality prevail. Since levelling doctrines are professed and no aristocracy is legally recognized, the individual who refuses to associate on equal terms with all other members of the community is an object of curiosity if not suspicion. If he must live by a trade or profession, he cannot hope to succeed as long as he refuses to join clubs and societies.

Like a church or any other society, the political party may be used as a social club through which a young man or woman may make valuable acquaintances and secure business, clients, or patients as the case may be. The social power of the party organization enables it to intrench itself by drawing into its ranks the best energies and talents of young people who, though by no means devoid of idealistic motives, cannot be blind to the stern necessities of the struggle for existence. In some cities, it is well for the young lawyer practicing in certain courts to be known as a prominent worker in the party to which the presiding judges belong. A Democratic doctor in a strongly Republican district of a Northern city would doubtless find his rise in the world somewhat handicapped if he were overzealous in the support of his party, and a belligerent Republican lawyer in a Southern city might very well find his business limited to practice in the federal courts. The subtle influences of party control are doubtless more powerful than the gross influences which appear upon the surface.

Equally elusive is the influence of the press and

propaganda. Nearly all newspapers are affiliated with political parties; even the avowedly independent papers are controlled by men affiliated with parties. Most political editorials are written with a party bias or with a view to party advantage. Even the news is colored more or less by party opinions. The emphasis given to events, the headlines, and the method of treatment reflect party pressures. During campaigns especially, the political atmosphere is charged with propaganda—printed, written, and oral. Even gossip, damaging or advantageous to candidates, sweeps like a whirlwind through party clubs and organizations. Someone has said that a party is "a great political whispering gallery."

Last, but not least, an effective practice, contributing to party strength, is the assistance given to the voters by the machine. Party leaders and workers favor the poor voters by a thousand charitable acts. They give outings, picnics, clam-bakes, and celebrations for them; they help the unemployed to get work with private corporations or in governmental departments; they pay the rent of sick and unfortunate persons about to be dispossessed; they appear in court for those in trouble, and often a word to the magistrate saves the voter from the workhouse or even worse; they remember the children at Christmas; and, in short, they are the ever watchful charity agents for their respective neighborhoods. A kind word and a little money in time of pressing need often will go further than an eloquent sermon on civic virtue. Thus politics as it operates through party organization is a serious and desperately determined business activity; it works night and day; it is patient; it gets what it can; it never relaxes.

Chapter II

Federalist-Republican Alignment

I T IS customary to separate American political history into three periods, using changes in party names as the basis of the division. According to this scheme, there have been three great party alignments since the formation of the Constitution: Federalists against Republicans (1789-1816), Whigs against Democrats (1830-1856), and Republicans against Democrats (1856 to the present time). Although the dates are merely approximate, they furnish useful chronological clues.

But this division is arbitrary and only for convenience. In fact, there has been no sharp break in the sources of party strength, in policy, or in opinion. On the contrary, these three alignments have been merely phases of one unbroken conflict originating in the age of George Washington and continuing without interruption to our own time.

§ *Federalist Measures*

The first of these alignments — Federalists against Republicans—was connected more or less directly with the contest over the framing and adoption of the federal Constitution.[1]

Authorities are generally agreed that the main support for the Constitution came from merchants, manufacturers, government bond holders, and other people of substantial property interests "along the line of the seaboard towns and populous regions." They are likewise agreed that the opposition came mainly from the inland farmers, debtors, and less prosperous sections of the country.[2]

The feelings aroused by the contest over the Constitution had not disappeared when the first administration was organized in 1789 with Washington as President and friends of the new system installed in all branches of the government—executive, legislative and judicial. With Alexander Hamilton, first Secretary of the Treasury, in the lead, the advocates of the new order, soon to be known as Federalists, carried through a series of

---

1. The roots of party antagonism lie deep in colonial times. In Virginia, there were contests between the upland farmers and the gentlemen planters of the seaboard before the seventeenth century closed. During the stirring prelude to the Revolution against Great Britain, the division between the Patriots and the Tories was supplemented by sharp divisions among the former. More than once the mechanics of the towns frightened the merchants by radical demands and serious rioting. All through the War of Independence, the revolutionists were split into radical and conservative factions—mechanics and poor farmers against the merchants and possessors of large property. See Beard, **Rise of American Civilization**, Vol. I, pp. 266-68.

2. Beard, **Economic Interpretation of the Constitution**, pp. 292-99, and **Economic Origins of Jeffersonian Democracy**, pp. 1-9.

economic measures which in time divided the country into two powerful parties. In summary form, these measures were as follows:

1. The funding of the national debt. All the old bonds, certificates, and other evidences of indebtedness issued by the Continental Congress during the Revolution were called in and new bonds for face value given to the holders.

2. The assumption of the revolutionary debts of the states. The federal government also called in the revolutionary debts of the states and issued new federal bonds instead; that is, the federal government assumed the obligations of the states and added them to the general debt of the nation.

These two operations, funding and assumption, deeply affected the purses of classes and masses. Before Hamilton began his work, the old bonds and notes issued during the Revolution had been selling at from ten to twenty cents on the dollar, because the national government and several states had failed to meet their obligations. During the dark days of uncertainty, a large part of this paper had been bought by speculators from the original holders at low prices with a view to profit taking. In the end, funding and assumption increased the value of the depreciated securities to the amount of approximately forty million dollars —a huge sum for those days. To raise the money to pay the interest on the debt, the federal government had to lay heavy taxes on the people, most of whom were farmers, not bondholders.

3. Protective tariff. The third measure on the Federalist program was the protection of American industries by the imposition of customs duties on imports coming into competition with American products. Hamilton openly favored an elaborate system of protection. Although his plans were not adopted in full, the first revenue bill passed in 1789 was mildly protective and, in time, other protective features were added.

4. The United States Bank. Under Hamilton's leadership, Congress chartered a banking corporation, authorized it to raise a large capital composed, three-fourths, of new federal bonds, and empowered it to issue currency and do a general banking business.

5. A sound national currency. Under the new Constitution, the states had to stop issuing paper money. The gold and silver coin of the United States now provided by law became the money of the country, with the notes of the United States Bank circulating on a parity.

6. Discrimination in favor of American shipping. To encourage the construction of an American merchant marine, Congress provided that the tonnage duties on foreign-built and foreign-owned ships should be five times as high as the duties on American ships. In line with this, other concessions were made to native shipping, especially that engaged in the China trade.

7. National defense. In creating a navy and a standing army, Congress had more in mind than the mere defense of the country against foreign foes. The navy was useful in protecting commerce on the high seas and the army in suppressing uprisings such as had occurred in Massachusetts in 1786. In other words, economic factors as well as patriotism were involved in the process.

8. Foreign affairs. When the wars of the French Revolution broke out in Europe, the Washington administration, largely inspired by Hamilton, frankly sympathized with England as against France and looked on the contest in the Old World as a conflict between property and order on the one side and democracy and anarchy on the other—akin in fact to the political dispute at home.

§ *The Rise of Opposition*

Now these measures were not excursions in theory. They were acts of power involving the pocketbooks of groups, affecting the distribution of wealth and the weight of classes in politics. Certainly the first six of them bore directly upon the economic interests of the citizens.

Under these laws, large sums of money were paid to the holders of government bonds who had been receiving little or nothing; people who were moderately well off one day found themselves rich the next. Under these laws, stockholders in the United States Bank earned handsome profits on their investment, protected manufacturers entered upon a period of prosperity, and merchants and money lenders were enabled, by the sound currency system and adequate judicial assistance, to carry on their operations safely in all parts of the country. Under these laws, heavy taxes were collected to pay the interest on the bonds and to maintain the new government.

Were these things done for beneficiaries at the expense of other classes, notably the farmers, or did the increased production caused by the operations more than cover the cost? On this point economists disagree and the historian cannot answer the question mathematically.

At all events, however, a considerable portion of the American people came to the conclusion that the Federalist measures and policies above enumerated in fact transferred money to investors, merchants, manufacturers, and the capitalistic interests in general, at the expense of the masses —a majority of whom were farmers and planters. "This plan of a National Bank is calculated to benefit a small part of the United States, the mercantile interest only; the farmers, the yeomanry, will derive no advantage from it," complained a member of Congress from Georgia. The protective tariff on steel will operate "as an oppressive, though indirect, tax upon agriculture," lamented a Congressman from Virginia. "The funding system was intended to effect what the Bank was contrived to accelerate: 1. Accumulation of great wealth in a few hands. 2. A political moneyed engine," protested another Virginia statesman.

In time, the citizens who took this view of the Hamiltonian program were marshalled, first as Anti-Federalists and later as Republicans, under the leadership of Thomas Jefferson, who was by occupation and opinion well fitted for his mission.

A planter, Jefferson was acquainted with the interests of agriculture. Moreover, he believed and said openly that "cultivators of the earth are the most valuable citizens. They are the most vigorous, the most independent, the most virtuous, and they are tied to their country and wedded to its liberty and interests by the most lasting bonds." In logical relation, he had a low opinion of commerce and industry, which created urban masses. "The mobs of great cities," he asserted, "add just so much to the support of pure government as sores do to the strength of the human body."

Holding such opinions, Jefferson set out to enlist a large following in his struggle against the capitalistic measures of Hamilton. He made his strongest appeal directly to the agriculturalists of the country. And when his party was fully organized he took pride in saying that "the whole landed interest is republican," that is, lined up on his side of the contest.

Speaking of the Federalists arrayed against him on the other side, Jefferson said that they included all the federal office holders, "all who want to be officers, all timid men who prefer the calm of despotism to the boisterous sea of liberty, British merchants and Americans trading on British capitals, speculators and holders in the banks and public funds, a contrivance invented for the purposes of corruption."

Appealing to the farmers and the masses in general against the larger capitalistic interests, Jefferson's party inevitably took a popular, that is, a democratic turn. This was in keeping with his theories, for he thought that kings, clergy, nobles, and other ruling classes of Europe had filled their countries with poverty and misery and kept the world in turmoil with useless wars. The common people, he reasoned, if given liberty and let alone, would be happier under their own government than under any ruling class.

To their economic arguments, the Jeffersonians added a constitutional theory. They declared that the Constitution did not give Congress the power to charter a bank, provide protection for manufacturers, and pass certain other measures sponsored by the Federalists. This was a "strict contruction" of the Constitution; that is, the powers of Congress were to be interpreted narrowly and the rights of the states liberally. Although the Federalists included in their ranks most of the leading men who had made the Constitution, they were thus accused of violating the very fundamental law which they had conceived and adopted. In this way, arose the wordy battle over the "true meaning" of the Constitution and the "rights of states" which occupies such a large place in the history of American political loquacity.

To the disputes over domestic questions were added differences of opinion about foreign policies. In the very spring in which Washington was inaugurated with such acclaim, the Estates General met at Versailles and opened the first scene in the great drama of the French Revolution; in 1791 a new constitution was put into effect and the power of the king was practically destroyed; the next year the first French republic was established; in 1793 Louis XVI was executed, and war was declared on England. These events were watched with deep interest by American citizens.

The more radical elements of the population, fresh from their own triumph over George III, remembered with satisfaction the execution of Charles I by their ancestors, and took advantage of the occasion to rejoice in the death of another ruler—the French monarch. A climax came in 1793, when France called on the United States to fulfill the terms of the treaty of 1778, in return for the assistance which had been given to the Americans in their struggle with England. The radicals wanted to aid France, either openly or secretly, in her war on England, but Washington and his conservative supporters refused to be drawn into the European controversy. So the Americans were divided into contending groups over foreign policy, and the division ran in the main along the line already cut by the Federalist-Republican contest over domestic questions.

§ *The Federalist-Republican Battle*

As the critics of the administration, known at first as Anti-Federalists, slowly changed from a mere opposition group into a regular party and took on the name Republican, the friends of the administration with Hamilton, John Jay, and John Adams in the lead, began to organize for political warfare under the banner of Federalism. In the third presidential election, the party alignment was complete. Jefferson, the leader of the Republicans, was roundly denounced as an atheist and leveler; while Adams, the Federalist candidate, was condemned by his opponents as "the monarchist." So sharply drawn was the contest that

Adams was chosen by the narrow margin of three electoral votes.

During Adams' administration, the Federalist party was thoroughly discredited. The Republican newspapers heaped indiscriminate abuse upon the head of the President and the Federalists generally. As a result Congress pushed through the Alien and Sedition Acts—the first authorizing the President to expel certain aliens deemed dangerous to the safety and peace of the country, and the second making the publication of attacks on any branch of the federal government a crime.

Under the Sedition Act, many Republicans were severely punished for trivial criticisms of the administration. For example, Callender, a friend of Jefferson, was convicted for saying, among other things: "Mr. Adams has only completed the scene of ignominy which Mr. Washington began." In letter and spirit the Act seemed contrary to the amendment to the federal Constitution guaranteeing freedom of press and speech against federal interference. At all events, the two laws called forth the famous Kentucky and Virginia Resolutions, and convinced even those moderately inclined towards democracy that Federalism meant the establishment of political tyranny. The death knell of the Federalist party was rung. Jefferson was elected in 1800 by a substantial majority over the Federalist candidate.

It has been the fashion to ascribe to the Federalists a political philosophy born of innate ill-will for the people. "Your people, sir," Hamilton is supposed to have said, "is a great beast"—as if in a burst of petulance.

Now this imputation is not entirely just. No doubt some of the emotions to which Federalists gave free vent were the feelings common to persons of large property—feelings of superiority and virtue. But there were practical grounds for distrusting "the people." Throughout the Revolution "the lower orders" had given trouble to the right wing of patriotism, threatening to upset the new ship of state before it was launched. Indeed, some blood had been shed in conflicts among the Patriots themselves before independence was won.

To the Tories who remained in America and rallied to the Federalist cause, the masses were, of course, contemptible in opinion and conduct. In the eyes of the Patriots of the right, the new democracy was responsible for the failure to pay the interest on the national and state debts between 1783 and 1789, for the refusal to grant aid and protection to American industry, for the uprising against the "rich and well-born" in Massachusetts in 1786, and for sundry other disturbances in the body politic. When, therefore, Federalists cursed the people—as they did in gross and in detail—they were not merely expressing a conservative temper. Rather were they reasoning, so they thought, from experience, bitter realistic experience at that.

CHAPTER III

TWENTY-EIGHT YEARS OF THE JEFFERSONIAN
PARTY

For twenty-eight years, from 1801 to 1829, Presidents calling themselves Republican occupied the White House—Jefferson, Madison, Monroe, and John Quincy Adams—and except for a short time at the beginning they were well supported in Congress by party members of their own persuasion. During this period, the Federalist party, as a national organization, died a lingering death. It continued to put up candidates until 1816, but after that failure it disappeared from the national theater. Deprived of a shelter all their own, active Federalists then went into the Republican organization and did what they could to bend it in their direction, while the intransigents of the old generation often sulked in their tents, lamenting the evil days upon which they had fallen.

Although they possessed the power of government, the Republicans, it must be said, did not have a perfectly free hand in carrying their policies into effect. For more than half of this period, the nations of Europe were engaged in the devastating Napoleonic wars which interfered with the shipment of American agricultural produce to Europe, and for a brief term the United States was at war with Great Britain. Owing to foreign events beyond their control, the Republicans were compelled to adopt many devices not to their liking, or at least contrary to their professions.

§ *Republican Economic Measures*

Nothing had caused more discussion among the Republicans than the national debt. Members of the extreme left had argued that it should be repudiated, that inasmuch as soldiers had given their lives to the revolutionary cause property owners should sacrifice their financial contributions. Not many, of course, held this extreme opinion, but some did, and the Federalists had attributed such views to the Republicans in general. A middle faction of Republicans opposed repudiation but thought that some reduction should be made in the generous terms adopted by Hamilton. All Republicans agreed that, in any case, the debt was a burden on the taxpayers, most of whom were farmers, that it was a source of speculation and corruption in Congress, and that it should be discharged in full as soon as possible.

Hence the Republicans paid off the national debt as fast as they could, and they were in a fair way to extinguish it when they got into a war with Great Britain in 1812 and were simply forced to increase it.

Hamilton's second great political institution, the United States Bank, likewise came in for its full share of Republican attack. On this point there was no compromise. In 1811, at the end of the twenty-year term, the charter of the Bank expired, and the Republicans refused to renew the life of the great "money power." The banking business passed into the hands of banks chartered by the states and the paper notes of these concerns flooded the country, some of them good, many of them bad.

If it had not been for a crisis, the Republicans probably would have stood firmly against any revival of the United States Bank. But during the war with Great Britain, which they undertook against the wishes of the business and commercial sections, they were driven into a corner in their efforts to pay their bills. In the end, they had to choose between surrendering to the private banks, which had sprung up in the business centers such as Boston, New York, and Philadelphia, and establishing a semi-political government bank under their own control. In the dilemma, they naturally chose the latter plan; in 1816 a Republican Congress chartered the second United States Bank and a Republican President approved it. Members on the left wing opposed this action and in growing numbers waged war on the new "money power." As we shall see, they split the party and destroyed the Bank. Even members of the middle and right factions accepted the Bank as a measure of necessity merely to save the government in their hands from a worse fate.

Into the tax program of the Republicans, the War of 1812 broke with incredible force. They had bitterly opposed the Federalists' direct taxes, which fell heavily upon land, and their internal taxes, especially the tax on whiskey which reached into the pockets of thousands of farmers who had little stills of their own. Once installed in office, the Republicans reduced and abolished until they cut the direct and internal revenue taxes and duties down almost to the vanishing point. These burdens so odious to agriculture had nearly disappeared when several of them had to be revived after war was declared on Great Britain. Wars cost money and somebody must pay for them! Yet it could be truly said that, until necessity compelled them to choose another course, the Republican statesmen had done their best to ease the taxes distasteful to their agricultural constituents.

Tariff schedules likewise became involved in war necessities. Those established under Federalist auspices were mildly protectionist in character. Hamilton's thorough-going program had been rejected by Congress. As the rates which the Republicans found in force on coming into office were light and yielded large revenues to pay off the hated debt, no radical changes were made in a downward direction.

On the contrary, the opposite happened. The wars in Europe, the War of 1812, the blockades, and the depredations played havoc with American farmers and planters. Unable to ship their produce abroad freely, they found it spoiling on their hands or sinking in price for the want of a market. Why not have a home market, therefore, beyond the reach of wars? Manufacturers approved the idea and offered to furnish the market for the produce of farms and plantations if they could get sufficient protection against foreign competition.

Despite loud protests on the left wing, the Republicans adopted in 1816 a protective tariff bill which would have delighted Hamilton had he been alive to see it. In a long oration, John C. Calhoun, a South Carolina planter, defended the bill in Congress on the ground that it would furnish a market for the produce of the soil. And the stoutest opposition came from New England whose shipping interests, engaged in a lucrative carrying trade, did not want foreign imports reduced by high tariffs. The business was economic but tables were reversed. As we shall see, when conditions changed, planters and farmers could alter their tariff policies. At no time did they forget to cherish the land.

Land—the source of Jefferson's party interest—also figured in two other strokes of policy made by the Republicans during this period. In 1803 they purchased the Louisiana Territory from Napoleon and thus added enough land to satisfy, it seemed, farmers and planters for a century or more. True to their class, the financial and commercial Federalists on the seaboard opposed the purchase on the ground that it would soon enable the agricultural interests of the South and West to dominate the country. That dominance was exactly what the Republicans wanted and, as they had a majority in Congress, the treaty of purchase was ratified.

The question of land similarly entered the War of 1812. According to the usual school-book traditions, this war was fought in defense of American rights against British depredations on the sea, but Professor Julius W. Pratt, in his *Expansionists of 1812,* has demolished that theory. Commercial interests were generally opposed to the war. Planters and farmers voted for it. The grand outcome was to be the annexation of the two Floridas for the planters and the annexation of Canada for the farmers. In the process, the Indian allies of Great Britain on the frontier were to be reduced to order so that pioneers could take up their abode in peace on the edges of American civilization. Owing to inadequate military preparations the plans failed.

The truth is that the Republicans did not believe in a powerful navy and a powerful standing army. In Jefferson's eyes, a navy was a costly Federalist device for which farmers and planters had to pay in taxes simply to protect the property of American shippers on the high seas.

Loyal to farmer traditions, Jefferson feared a strong regular army. It was expensive, he thought, and unnecessary because the popular militia could be relied upon to keep order and defend the country. Although Jefferson used the navy with vigor and telling effect on the Barbary pirates, he and his party reduced rather than strengthened the regular armed forces of the country. The failure to achieve their ends in the War of 1812 may be laid at their door. Farmers did not realize that banking and fighting were professions that could not be learned overnight.

On the whole, it could be said that the Republicans were loyal to the landed interest which they frankly championed in politics. Most of their apparent veerings in the Federalist direction were due to that loyalty rather than to any conversion of heart.

§. *Republican Political Theory.*

In the development of political theory, the Republicans proceeded with considerable directness.

On the side of ceremony, their task was easy. For various reasons the Federalists had wanted to surround the government with pomp and circumstance. Many of them were old Tories who had enjoyed prostrating themselves before the monarchy and the church in the days of King George.

Some of them were rich and idle, and could not think of anything more diverting than presidential balls, receptions, and etiquette. Others, taking a more utilitarian view, looked upon parades, lace, gold braid, brass buttons, spangles, horse hair, and robes as useful things to awe "the mob," give it respect for government, and keep it on its knees. Since a number of Jefferson's followers were among the people called "the mob" by Federalists and since farmers did not as a rule care for ceremony, the Republicans laid great stress on simplicity and abandoned many of the ceremonial precedents set by Washington and Adams. Jefferson once stopped at a boarding house and walked to the capitol for his inauguration! "Jeffersonian simplicity" was a great slogan for succeeding generations, even though Jefferson lived lavishly most of his life.

This doctrine of simplicity, in fact, fitted well into the larger Jeffersonian creed of "the less government the better"—a creed likewise adapted to the primitive agricultural life of the country. Lest there be some doubt about his political philosophy on this score, Jefferson was careful to make a full statement in his very first inaugural. Besides praising religious liberty, majority rule, freedom of press, "the encouragement of agriculture and of commerce as its handmaid," the diffusion of information, and the "supremacy of the civil over the military authority," Jefferson clearly described his political ideal: "a wise and frugal Government which shall restrain men from injuring one another, shall leave them otherwise free to regulate their own pursuits of industry and improvement and shall not take from the mouth of labor the bread it has earned. This is the sum of good government and this is necessary to close the circle of our felicities." In a word, here is the whole gospel of *laissez faire,* no government in business, so appropriate to simple agriculture, and, half a century later, as a curious fate would have it, to the requirements of manufacturers in resisting factory legislation.

With a similar pertinence to reality, the Republicans championed intellectual freedom. They had suffered severely at the hands of the Federalists under the Sedition Act, and they refused, when in power, to make use of the instrumentality they had previously condemned, until slavery—the labor basis of the planting system—was menaced by agitation.

In harmony with their general theories, but also

resting on practical grounds, was the Republican creed respecting the judiciary. Believing in majority rule, Jefferson held that it was absurd and contrary to the Constitution to give to the federal judiciary the right to declare acts of Congress null and void, that is, as he put it, the right to prescribe rules for the government of the legislative and executive branches.

Beyond theory lay realities. A Federalist justice of the Supreme Court, Samuel Chase, had been particularly active in denouncing from the bench "dangerous democratic doctrines," and the Republicans attempted to oust him by impeachment. Defeated in this effort by the Senate, they were all the more convinced in their opposition to what has been called "judicial supremacy." If they showed any tendency to relax, they were likely to be aroused again by a ringing decision against state rights by Chief Justice Marshall, a doughty Federalist whom the Federalists put on the bench for life just as Jefferson came to power for a term.

Only on one important point of political theory did the Republicans reverse themselves in practice. When they were opposing Hamilton's economic program, they held that the Constitution should be strictly construed, that the federal gov-

[53]

ernment could not do anything which the Constitution did not clearly authorize. However, when they came to exercising power themselves they were not seriously troubled by such strait-laced views. The Constitution certainly did not say anything about buying more territory; yet the Republicans bought Louisiana with great rejoicing. Jefferson thought the transaction unconstitutional, but lawyers found a warrant for it in the clause giving the President and Senate the right to make treaties. In any case, it took a liberal eye to find it.

With equal facility the Federalists, once loose constructionists, now that tables were turned, took a strict view of the Constitution. Since they were in the opposition, nearly everything Republican was "unconstitutional"—the embargo, the Louisiana Purchase, and conscription for the War of 1812, for example. If their speeches are to be taken literally, they were in great distress lest the Constitution be violated by the free interpretation made by Republicans.

Reviewing this reversal of political theory by both parties, a cynic might say that circumstances alter opinions and laugh softly at the constitutional eloquence of lawyers. But a fairer judgment would be that actions which we approve never appear in the same light as actions which we dislike. At all events, "strict interpretation" received a severe jolt at the hands of its authors and never wore the same aspect again.

If the Republicans grew a bit "loose" in their constitutional theories while they were in power, they at least contributed one fairly definite article of political faith, namely, the idea that no President should serve more than two terms. Washington had declined a third term—not because he thought it unconstitutional or contrary to political wisdom. The fact was that he had served his country for many long years and was in need of a well-earned rest. Jefferson was also thoroughly weary in 1809 and did not want a third term on any conditions, but he made a kind of philosophy out of his preference, saying: "General Washington set the example of voluntary retirement after eight years. I shall follow it. And a few more precedents will oppose the obstacle of habit to anyone after awhile who shall endeavor to extend his term. Perhaps it will beget a disposition to establish it by an amendment of the Constitution."

Rustic simplicity, *laissez faire,* freedom of opinion, a critical attitude toward the judiciary, a strict but convenient interpretation of the Constitution, and the third term doctrine—such were the chief political articles among the professions of Jeffersonian Republicans.

CHAPTER IV

NATIONAL REPUBLICAN (WHIG)-DEMOCRATIC
ALIGNMENT

§ *The Changing Economic Order*

DURING the long years of Republican supremacy, certain fundamental economic changes occurred, which strengthened the left wing of that party. These great changes were connected with the settlement of the Northwest Territory, the extension of cotton culture into the Southwest, and the revolution wrought in Eastern industry by machinery.

In the process, the balance of power was shifted from the seaboard states to the West. Kentucky was admitted to the Union in 1792, Tennessee in 1796, Ohio in 1803, Louisiana in 1812, Indiana in 1816, Illiniois in 1818, Mississippi in 1817, Alabama in 1819, and Missouri in 1821.

In these Western states there arose a type of economic society such as had never before appeared in the history of the world, at least on a large scale. A vast region was settled by hardy and restless pioneers who crossed the mountains, cut down the forests, built houses, and founded homes. In the possession of this world's goods they were, for the most part, substantially equal; it was easy to acquire land; any thrifty and industrious farmer with his family could readily secure the comforts of a rude but healthful and independent life. Practically every white man could vote. In the log cabins were developed political ideas fundamentally different from those entertained by the rich merchants of the East or the aristocratic land-holders in the manors along the Hudson.

In the West, the leveling theories of Jefferson were fairly realized. Owing to the simple life which farmers lived, government was to them a simple thing; anyone could hold the office of sheriff, county clerk, road supervisor, state auditor, or governor. Since the duties of the offices were easily understood and the emoluments connected with them attractive, especially to men who earned their bread with the ax and the plow, the Western settlers seized with eagerness upon the doctrine of short terms and rotation in office.

Needing capital to develop their resources and provide means of transportation, these Western people were always borrowers in the money market. Of necessity, they had to depend largely upon Eastern financiers for credits and, being far from the center of business, they had to pay high rates of interest on their loans. In the best of times they were hard driven and during depressions they were plunged into distress. Naturally they sought a remedy for their difficulties and came to the conclusion that it consisted in currency inflation—perhaps through the agency of state banks empowered to issue bills of credit. By such a device they hoped to pay their debts more easily and to command a higher price for their produce —economic operations which threw them into opposition to creditors and buyers.

No less significant for politics than the development of the West was an economic revolution in the agricultural system of the South created by invention of textile machinery and the cotton gin. With the extraordinary demand for cotton came a demand for more land to cultivate and more slaves for labor. The slave population now rapidly increased and the lust for money seized the dominant planting class as it had seized the mill owners of New England. Under the old plantation system, masters and slaves dwelt side by side from generation to generation, mitigating the bondage of slavery by a somewhat patriarchal relation, but under the new system slaves were worked in gangs with less regard for humane considerations, and the profit-making motive swept everything before it. Once condemned or merely condoned, slavery was now defended as "a positive good," and inevitably drew to its support the best intellectual strength of the South.

During these crowded years, the East as well as the West and South was being transformed. The industries of New England and the Middle States, founded in colonial times and fostered by a protective tariff especially after the war of 1812, began their spectacular career. Mechanics from England came to America in large numbers, bringing with them the designs of machines which had recently wrought a revolution in English industry. In 1807, Fulton inaugurated steam navigation on the Hudson; and far and wide hamlets were expanded into manufacturing centers through the magic of steam. The tide of immigration from Europe steadily increased, and most immigrants found their homes in the growing cities of the East. In the twenty years from 1800 to 1820, the population of Boston almost doubled, while that of New York rose from 60,000 to 123,700. Owing to the property qualifications placed on the suffrage by the constitutions of the Eastern states, most of the immigrants and native workers in the factories were excluded in the beginning from the right to vote; but before the first quarter of the nineteenth century had elapsed, the restrictions on the suffrage had been broken down by popular agitation.

§ *Jackson's Left-wing Movement*

Here were the changed social conditions which made the United States of 1825 as different from the United States of Washington's day as the England of Cobden and Bright was different from the England of Bolingbroke and Walpole. The financial and industrial interests of New England and the Middle States had now aligned against them the laboring classes, the farmers of the West, and the slave owners who raised cotton principally for the British market.

In 1828, there was found a standard-bearer who, curiously enough, seemed to represent these three diverse elements. That was Andrew Jackson, a resident of Tennessee, a bold frontiersman, immensely popular on account of his victory over the English at New Orleans and his unqualified championship of what he called "the rights of the people." Triumphantly elected, and feeling behind him the irresistible pressure of popular support, he began an executive policy which seemed for a time to transfer the seat of government from the capitol to the White House. He adopted the most novel notions about the rights of the President under the Constitution; he ousted old office-holding "aristocrats" without regard to appearances and circumstances, and gave their places to his friends and supporters; he destroyed the United States Bank, the stronghold of powerful financial interests, in spite of the opposition raised up against him in Congress; and when nullification appeared in South Carolina, he issued a ringing proclamation which showed that he was a stanch defender of nationalism as against state's rights. During his two administrations, the Republicans gradually dropped their old name and proudly assumed the title of Democrats—a word that savored of anarchy a generation before and was then abhorred by most respectable people.

In short, Jackson, a representative of the agrarian South and West, ardently supported by the working classes in the East, took his place firmly in the left wing of the party started by Jefferson. His position with respect to the main Federalist institutions and articles of political faith makes this evident beyond argument.

The Federalists, besides funding the national debt, looked upon it as an excellent permanent device for drawing moneyed men to the support of the government. Jeffersonian Republicans, on the other hand, had done their best to get rid of the debt by paying it off, but the necessities of the War of 1812 had piled it up again. In his first annual message, Jackson favored the extinction of the entire debt by payment, rejoiced that the moment for extinction was at hand, and reached this goal before he went out of office.

Second on the Federalist list was the United States Bank. On the expiration of its charter in 1811, the Republicans destroyed it, but during the financial distress created by the War of 1812 they had been forced to re-establish it. For that reversal their radical followers never forgave them, and early in his administration Jackson opened a battle on this engine of "the money power." He practically demolished it by a drastic use of executive authority and finished the work by preventing a renewal of its charter in Congress.

From the beginning, Federalist businessmen and statesmen had insisted on a sound national currency, including notes of the Bank circulating on a parity with gold and silver. Republican philosophers on the right opposed the issue of paper money on the ground that it added nothing to the wealth of the country. As they thought, the bankers, with government sanction, merely used the printing press liberally to manufacture notes which were lent to the public at six per cent interest or more—a very profitable transaction for the bankers. But Republican philosophers on the left, while bitterly opposing the United States Bank currency, favored a more generous issue of notes by state banks, on the theory that they could pay their debts easier and sell their produce at higher prices if a great deal of money was afloat. Jackson likewise favored banks under state supervision. Judges appointed by him interpreted the Constitution in such a fashion as to permit states to charter banks, hold the stock, and issue money—a very ingenious way of avoiding the constitutional provision to the effect that states could not make anything but gold and silver legal tender in the payment of debts. In their paper money practices, the Jacksonian Democrats went beyond the Constitution back to the time of Daniel Shays.

With respect to the protective tariff, Jackson was true to Republican theory when he said that "it is principally as manufactures and commerce tend to increase the value of agricultural productions . . . that they deserve the fostering care of government." But he vaguely added that they deserved such fostering care because they catered to the "wants and comforts of society." This uncertainty the Democrats later cured by reducing the tariff drastically in the direction of a revenue basis. None of them wanted to abolish the tariff entirely for that would have brought about direct taxation on land, an alternative not pleasant to farmers and planters.

Federalists boasted of having "the rich and well-born" in their ranks. Jackson, in waging war on the Bank, made himself the open champion of "the humbler members of society—the farmers, mechanics, and laborers" against "the rich and powerful."

Faithful to the Jeffersonian tradition, Jackson looked upon the federal judiciary with a critical eye. He refused to accept as binding upon himself the decision of the Supreme Court upholding the constitutionality of the United States Bank. "Mere precedent," he said, "is a dangerous source of authority, and should not be regarded as deciding questions of constitutional power, except where the acquiescence of the people and the states can be considered well settled."

More than once he defied the Court by refusing to execute its mandates and in one case he is reported to have said: "John Marshall has made his decision:—now let him enforce it."

§ *National Republican-Whig Combination*

Holding strongly to such opinions and commanding wide popular support among farmers and mechanics, Jackson seemed to be sovereign in Washington; but nevertheless the factions opposed to his policies steadily gained in unity and power. The banking and financial interests of the East had every reason to fear that a calamity would follow the destruction of the United States Bank and the flooding of the country with paper money through the state banks; many members of his party in the South, who sympathized with the nullification policy of South Carolina, violently attacked Jackson for his determined stand against the action of that state. Furthermore, there was a well-organized group of Eastern manufacturers who wanted to extend the system of protective tariffs beyond the point to which Jackson was willing to go. In addition to this host of enemies, Jackson raised up against himself many disappointed office-seekers, as well as the old office-holders whom he had turned out. There was also in the West a growing number of persons who wanted to secure larger federal grants for internal improvements— roads, harbors, canals, and river facilities—than he was willing to concede.

These elements of opposition to Jackson were finally brought together in a new organization. Making use of a clever vote-catching device, they called themselves National Republicans, and nominated for the presidency in 1831 Jackson's powerful foe, Henry Clay, of Kentucky. In its platform of that year, the party declared in favor of "an adequate protection to American industry," "a uniform system of internal improvements sustained and supported by the general government," "the preservation of the authority and jurisdiction" of the Supreme Court, and the maintenance of the Senate as "preëminently a conservative branch of the federal government." Defeated on this straightforward Federalist program, the National Republicans widened their base and about 1834 merged into a more miscellaneous collection calling themselves "Whigs"—a title taken from English politics, signifying antagonism to high executive prerogative. Marshalled under this banner, they appealed to everybody who was discontented with Jackson.

Nominally the Whig party lasted until the close of the presidential campaign of 1856. It enjoyed two brief periods of triumph. In 1840, without having made any declaration of principles at all, it elected William Henry Harrison, a military hero. After a second defeat four years later, with Clay as the candidate, the party once more resorted to the old device and in 1848 carried the day with another popular hero, General Taylor. Even this design failed the Whigs the next time, for their third military hero, General Scott, was utterly routed.

Operating in a country predominantly agricultural, the Whigs had to be circumspect in their conduct. Their choice of military heroes as candidates lent confusion to the period, but there was no doubt about the measures which the Whig leaders cherished in their hearts. In their program, the Federalist creed was repeated in full or rather, it would be more correct to say, continued unbroken. Indeed, many a Federalist of the old school who had held his nose during the years of Republican supremacy under the Jeffersonians and during Democratic uproar under Jackson lived to rejoice in the election of Harrison in 1840. Nor should it be forgotten that Daniel Webster, the hope and pride of the Whigs, "the merchants' pet," as he was dubbed by Democrats, began his career as a Federalist. His father was a Federalist and "it is said, being taken sick in a Democratic town had himself removed lest he should·die in such pollution." The great Daniel himself, loyal to his early discipline, fired his first political gun in 1804 by writing a pamphlet showing the virtues of Federalism and the vices of Democracy.

Upholding the Hamilton tradition, the Whigs placed the protection of American industry high among the objects to be attained by political action. Words they followed by deeds. Although the tariff compromise of 1833, which temporarily "scotched" secession in South Carolina, was a sort of gentlemen's agreement to regulate rates downward according to a sliding scale, the Whigs, with the aid of Democrats from special sections, broke the understanding and raised the rates in 1842. A cry of rage went up from the planters, but the Whigs were determined and in a hurry.

In attempting to restore the second Federalist institution—the United States Bank—the Whigs were not so fortunate. But their defeat on this issue was due to the death of President Harrison a short time after his inauguration—not to any lack of will on their part. They were prepared to re-establish the Bank and were simply outwitted by Harrison's successor, John Tyler, a Virginia politician nominated for the vice-presidency to catch Democratic votes in the South. With their defeat on this issue, their designs for a sound currency system also fell to the ground.

Displaying a zeal that delighted the Chief Justice, John Marshall, the Whig forerunners, the National Republicans, as we have seen, came to the moral support of the federal judiciary, so vigorously attacked by Jefferson and Jackson. As a matter of fact, Marshall hoped that Clay would be elected in 1832 so that he could resign with the assurance that a "proper" successor would take his place. It was the second triumph of Jackson that kept him on the bench until that still more invincible leveller, Death, finally removed him from the scene. But for nearly two decades, Webster lived to defend "the good old doctrines" handed down by the Fathers against sappers and miners on the left.

That other interest dear to the Federalists—commerce—was also steadily supported in every direction by the Whigs. It was under Whig auspices that the movement for subsidizing mail steamers on the high seas was inaugurated, culminating in the subsidy act of March 3, 1845. It was mainly with Whig support that this act was maintained and extended. It was under a Democratic President, James Buchanan, that notice of "complete abrogation of contracts" for such subsidies was served on American shipping interests in 1859.

Less hampered by Democratic opposition in the field of executive action, the Whigs, whenever in possession of the presidency, used the Navy and the State Department to advance the sale of manufactured goods in the Far East and other places in the Pacific where agencies of power could be plied with effect. It was under Whig direction that formal relations were established with China in

1844, that Japan was broken open by Commodore Perry ten years later, and that the governments of the Old World were warned against trespassing on American preserves in Hawaii—all foreshadowing the days of William McKinley. In other words, the Whigs believed that the flag went before and after trade and understood the nature of commercial empires.

§ *The Fruits of Democratic Triumph*

Between 1828 and 1860 the Democrats won every presidential election except two, and during most of that period they controlled Congress. Not long after the death of Marshall, they got complete possession of the Supreme Court. The numerical supremacy of farmers and planters seemed to promise an indefinite lease of power. If conservative planters had little liking for the leveling doctrines of Jacksonian Democracy, they were practical men and finally became convinced that they could only hope to hold their own in politics against advancing industrialism by an alliance with farmers.

On fundamentals of economic action the two wings of agriculture were long able to agree. In fact, while the Whigs were trying to get possession of the government by nominating military heroes and avoiding a clear statement of principles, the Democrats were making their doctrines more and more precise.

In their platform of 1840, they wrote their agrarian creed in language so plain that any farmer or mechanic could understand it. They opposed protective tariffs, the establishment of another United States Bank, internal improvements, the creation of public debts, and all interference with slavery—the labor supply of the planters. At every presidential election until 1860, the Democrats repeated this profession of economic faith, and in every presidential campaign their orators refined it.

In practice, the Democrats carried out most of their promises. They defeated every attempt to restore the Bank which Jackson had destroyed. They struck a smashing blow at the protective tariff in their revenue law of 1846 and again in 1857, indicating their determination to destroy the Hamiltonian system root and branch. In 1859, the last of the subsidies for transatlantic steamships was ordered discontinued by Congress, and shippers were given to understand that they were to receive no such favors from the federal government. In the meantime, as the Federalist members of the Supreme Court, with Justice Marshall at their head, passed away, Democrats were appointed to take their places; and Hamilton's theories about the Constitution were generally abandoned in favor of the rights of states. In particular, the clause of the Constitution forbidding states to issue paper money—bills of credit—was reinterpreted in such a way as to permit states to set up banks which flooded the country with paper currency; and the clause respecting the obligation of contracts was practically destroyed by new judicial reasoning.

Loyal to the anti-commercial sentiments of Jefferson, the Democrats were indifferent to various proposals made in the middle period for using the Navy to occupy strategic trading posts in the Pacific and the Far East; but they were not partisans of a "little America." On the contrary, as the party of planters and farmers, they were advocates of that kind of expansion which yielded more land for slave owners and freeholders. They brought Texas into the Union in 1845, and waged a war on Mexico which ended in magnificent additions of land in 1848, in spite of opposition from the Whig side. If it had not been for resistance in that quarter, the Democrats would have probably annexed Cuba and huge slices of Latin-America on the mainland and in the Caribbean, thus strengthening the landed interest founded on slave labor. To the influence of Whig opposition must be added that of many free farmers enrolled under the Democratic banner, who feared and sometimes disliked the dominance of the slave-holding planters in their partnership.

CHAPTER V.

DEMOCRATIC-REPUBLICAN ALIGNMENT

WHILE the Democrats were refusing to support industrial enterprise, vital economic forces were preparing the way for an intensification of the battle between agriculture and capitalism. To what extent was the development of these forces due to political action, to party conflicts? No one can answer in exact terms. Certainly in a large measure, they expressed the inherent vitality of the people engaged in the pursuit of economic goods. It is equally certain that they strengthened the Hamilton-Webster, the Federalist-Whig, side of the political line-up.

§ *Shifts in the Economic Setting*

In the Northeast, manufacturing and railways were rapidly expanding, employing more labor and increasing the number and wealth of businessmen. By 1850, the value of the property employed in mills, mines, railways, and urban undertakings generally exceeded the value of all the farms and plantations between the Atlantic and the Pacific. A fact immense and ominous, as Carlyle would say.

In the South, cotton planting, stimulated by the development of the cotton gin and textile machinery, became the dominant interest, as against tobacco, rice, and sugar; by 1860 nearly two-thirds of the slaves were engaged in cultivating that crop. Cotton raising rapidly exhausted the soil and led the planters to push steadily westward, occupying new land.

In the Northwest, farmers were pressing across the Mississippi, demanding the opening of more territories to the plow and the granting of free homesteads to all who cared to ask for them. There was also a rapid growth in industrial cities like Cincinnati and Chicago and in the construction of railways uniting the Mississippi Valley with the Atlantic ports of Philadelphia, New York, and Boston. Once the stronghold of Jacksonian Democracy, the Northwest was now being assimilated to the economic system of the Northeast—severed from its affiliation with the Southern planters.

§ *The Slavery Issue*

Into the issues inherited from Hamilton's day— the tariff, bank, internal improvements, sound currency, and subsidies for business enterprise—was now injected a new issue, slavery. In 1831, William Lloyd Garrison launched his campaign against slavery, denouncing it as sinful and immoral. Twelve years later, a Free Soil party was organized to oppose the extension of bondage into the territories and three times it presented candidates for the presidency.

But neither the abolitionists nor the Free Soilers made much headway against the popular current. The former never started a political party and in the election of 1852 the latter polled only 156,000 votes out of more than four million votes cast. Had the abolition question stood alone and had the slave owners been content with maintaining slavery in the states where it was lawful, the controversy over the subject might never have taken a serious turn.

It so happened, however, that slavery could not be isolated. It was a labor system, the basis of planting, the foundation of the Southern aristocracy. And that aristocracy, being agricultural in

[78]

interest, generally opposed high protective tariffs, ship subsidies, internal improvements, and other measures deemed advantageous to business enterprise.

Moreover, that aristocracy, eager to protect itself against adverse legislation at Washington, was constantly afraid of being out-voted in Congress. Especially did it object to the exclusion of slavery from the territories because that policy meant the erection of new free states to "overbalance" the Southern states.

Declaring that the Western territories had all been won by common sacrifices, Southern planters never ceased to regard it an act of justice to open the West to slavery. Although they accepted the Missouri Compromise of 1820 excluding slavery from the northern portion of the Louisiana territory and the compromise of 1850, their most ardent leaders refused to abide by the settlement as final.

At last, in 1854, they came out boldly with their demand. Under the leadership of Stephen A. Douglas, supported by an almost solid delegation from the South, Congress, in that year, passed the Kansas-Nebraska Act which expressly repealed the Missouri Compromise and provided that two western territories then erected, Kansas and Nebraska, could come into the Union as states with or without slavery, as their constitutions might stipulate.

§ *Rise of the Third Republican Party*

On the very morning after the House of Representatives took up the Kansas-Nebraska bill, several members of that body held a conference and agreed that the "slave power" could only be checked by the formation of a party directly opposed to its plans for expansion. About the same time a mass meeting was held at Ripon, Wisconsin, and a resolution adopted to the effect that a new organization, to be called Republican, should be formed on the question of slavery extension, if the bill passed.

Indeed, all through the North and East, there were signs of dissolution among the Democrats and Whigs, and a general re-alignment; in the spring and summer of 1854, meetings were held in Illinois, Maine, Vermont, Michigan, Iowa, Indiana, Massachusetts, and New York, at which the Kansas-Nebraska bill was roundly denounced. On July 6, 1854, a state convention was held at

Jackson, Michigan, at which a full state ticket of Republican candidates was nominated.

Thus launched, a third Republican party—bearing the vote-getting title which Jefferson had given to his hosts in 1800 and Clay's party had taken in 1831—held its first national convention at Philadelphia in June, 1856, on a call issued by a preliminary meeting assembled at Pittsburg, in the preceding February. At this convention, John Charles Frémont was nominated as the candidate on a platform which declared that it was the right and duty of Congress to prohibit slavery in the territories. In the campaign which ensued. Frémont won 1,341,264 votes against 2,712,703 votes cast in favor of the Democratic and the Whig candidates.

During the four years which followed, the Republican party gained in strength. It gathered recruits among Northern farmers and mechanics, who believed that the federal lands should be given away in homesteads to poor men. It added to its farmer and mechanic regiments, manufacturers of the East who objected strenuously to the reduction of the protective tariff by the Democrats in 1857, and demanded an increase in the rates.

Responding to the requirements of these powerful groups, the Republicans, at their convention in Chicago in 1860, favored a homestead law and a protective tariff, as well as the exclusion of slavery from the territories. Thus they appealed to many farmers and mechanics who had formerly voted the Democratic ticket and at the same time made a bid for support among the Whig manufacturers who clung to the doctrines of Alexander Hamilton. By selecting as their candidate, Abraham Lincoln, of Illinois, they made a shrewd and fateful stroke.

Fortunately for the Republicans, the Democrats now split into two factions, one headed by Stephen A. Douglas, who hoped to solve the slavery question by allowing the people of each territory, on admission to the Union as a state, to decide it for themselves; the other by John C. Breckinridge, who held to the extreme Southern view that Congress had no power to prevent slavery in the territories. By another faction composed of conservative Whigs and Democrats, known as Constitutional Unionists, John Bell was nominated on a platform that begged the slavery issue. Owing to the division among their opponents, the Republicans were able to win the presidency, although their popular vote was only 1,866,452 as against 2,815,617 cast for their opponents.

§ *A Federalist Program under Republican Auspices*

During the Civil War and Reconstruction, the Republicans repudiated the policies which the Democrats had laboriously supported between 1830 and 1860, and substituted other policies more in accord with the historic principles of the Federalists and the Whigs, thus illustrating again the essential continuity of the American political battle. At the close of the civil conflict, the Republicans were in a position similar to that of the Federalists in Hamilton's day, with respect to nearly all fundamental issues.

1. National debt. The Federalists had funded and defended a great national debt, drawing the creditors to the support of the federal government. In 1865, the Republicans had a war debt more than twenty times the size of Hamilton's accumulation, and all holders of federal bonds looked to the Republican party for the strict payment of interest and principal. The old Jefferson-Jackson

idea of a debtless government seemed far removed
again.

2.   Protective tariff. After many years of de-
bate and agitation, the Democrats, by 1857, had
pushed the tariff far down the scale in the direction of free trade. During their tenure of power
from 1861 to 1865, the Republicans more than
realized the Hamiltonian ideal by raising the
duties again and again, to the highest peak of
protection yet reached in the history of the
country.

3.   Banking system. With respect to no issue
had the Democrats been more consistent than in
dealing with the United States Bank. Jeffersonian Republicans had been against it and had only
yielded to a demand for its restoration in 1816
under the necessities of war finance. In Jackson's
administration, the Bank was completely demolished and the most heroic efforts of the Whigs
could not revive it. But in 1863—once more in
time of war distress—the third Republican party
managed to create another national banking system, drawing to the support of the government a
powerful economic interest.

4.   Currency. When the Civil War broke out,
the country was flooded with paper money issued

by local banks chartered by the states. There were hundreds of varieties of all denominations, some sound, but much of it depreciated and fluctuating.

This was a condition of affairs akin to that which the Fathers encountered when they set up the Constitution and inaugurated the federal government. It was disturbing to business and pleased only debtors and farmers. Returning to Hamiltonian principles in 1865, the Republicans abolished this state currency by taxing it out of existence. Unfortunately, however, for the cause of sound money, they had to issue huge quantities of paper themselves to finance the war; but a few years later they put it all on a specie basis.

5. The commercial empire. The extension of trading operations, particularly in the Pacific and the Far East, which the Federalists had favored with special legislation and the Whigs had promoted by vigorous executive action through the Navy and State Departments, was not overlooked even during the dark days of the Civil War.[1]

William H. Seward, whom Lincoln selected as head of the State Department, was the most outspoken imperialist in the country. During the campaign of 1860 he had proclaimed the future of

---

1. See above, p. 71.

the American empire. Canada was to be annexed, our southern borders were to be pushed down to include Latin-American republics, the Pacific was announced as the theatre of the coming centuries, and a conflict between the United States and Russia on the plains of China was prophesied as a fruit of destiny. Such was the creed of the master in charge of foreign affairs from 1861 until 1869.

Fantastic as most of Seward's doctrines may have appeared in 1860, they were not all mere rhetoric. Some of them took practical form within a few years. When the Pacific railway was authorized in the very midst of the civil conflict, its value to merchants engaged in Far Eastern trade, as well as its importance to the Union, was recognized by the initiated. In 1867, Seward purchased Alaska from Russia, carrying the frontier of the United States near to the Asiatic shore. About the same time, through the good offices of the Navy Department, Seward arranged for the acquisition of a naval base in Santo Domingo, for the purchase of the Virgin Islands, and for American control over the Isthmus of Panama. In these three undertakings he was defeated by opposition in Congress where such designs were not yet fully understood.

But his schemes were not forgotten. In 1869, President Grant arranged for the annexation of Santo Domingo, only to be baffled by Congress; to the end of his administration Grant favored the project on the ground, as he said himself, that "the soil would soon have fallen into the hands of United States capitalists." In 1872, an American naval officer secured a coaling station from a local prince in Samoa far away in the South Seas. In 1875, a treaty with the ruler of Hawaii bound him not to alienate any of his territory except to the United States and a few years later a supplementary treaty gave the United States exclusive use of Pearl Harbor. Thus it could be said that the managers in the party of Hamilton, Webster, and Seward were consistent in their solicitude for commercial and naval empire and prepared the way for the administration of William McKinley, which finally let mankind know, what was already a fact, that America was a world power.

6. Judicial supremacy. From its Jeffersonian forerunner, the Democratic party, with its theory of majority rule, had inherited a tradition of criticism with respect to the federal judiciary. In the middle period, however, after all the old Federalist judges had died or resigned and good Demo-

crats had been appointed to the bench, the tradition faded. When the Supreme Court, in the Dred Scott case (1857) upheld slavery in the territories, Democrats demanded unqualified loyalty and obedience to the decisions of that great tribunal. It was the new Republican party, whose anti-slavery plank had been splintered by the decision, that now criticised the Court and talked about "reconstructing" it. But once more time and politics worked a reorganization of the Court and Republicans conveniently forgot their former resolutions of protest against its actions.

They even effected a revision of the Constitution which gave the federal judiciary a power over the states far greater than it had ever enjoyed. Before they took over the government in 1861, the Supreme Court, in the hands of Democratic judges, had practically destroyed, by ingenious reasoning, the provisions of the original Constitution imposing restraints on the states, and thus left them free to tax, issue paper money through banks, modify contracts, change the charters of corporations, and otherwise interfere "unduly" with business enterprise. This challenge the Republicans met. By the Fourteenth Amendment, adopted in 1868, after military compulsion had been applied to certain Southern states, they provided that no state should ever deprive any person of life, liberty, or property without due process of law.

Although the immediate occasion of this Amendment was the granting of civil rights to the newly emancipated slaves, it was the intention of the framers to apply it broadly to other persons and corporations. In due time hundreds of state laws interfering with capitalistic undertakings were declared null and void by the judiciary acting under the terms of the Fourteenth Amendment.

7. Free land for farmers and mechanics. While the Republicans were effecting these important economic reforms, they fulfilled a promise made to farmers and mechanics in their platform of 1860. By the Homestead Act of 1862, they offered a farm of 160 acres from the national domain, free of all charges except petty fees, to citizens and aliens who had declared their intention of becoming citizens. Applicants merely had to comply with certain conditions in order to secure full ownership. Thus to the Republican party hundreds of thousands of farmers in the West were indebted for the very soil they tilled, and nothing

short of a crisis could make them forget their obligation.

This union of businessmen and free farmers could function rather smoothly now that the Democratic planters were ruined by the Civil War. Defeated on the field of battle, deprived of their slaves by abolition, and for a long time governed under military authority from Washington, the planters could not recover their former position of power in the Democratic party. Even after the wounds of the War were healed, this important agricultural group, once the bulwark of the landed interest, did not regain its old place of continuous dominance in politics. Giant industry, marching in seven-league boots, outstripped it in the race.

§ *Years of Republican Supremacy*

From the period of Civil War and Reconstruction the Republicans emerged as a powerful, consolidated party fortified by an intense patriotism, by the support of the manufacturing interests which had flourished under the war tariffs, by the patronage of capitalists eager to swing forward with the development of railways and new enterprises, and by farmers grateful for many favors, including homesteads. In possession of all the important offices, controlling the federal legislature, executive, and judiciary, with the Democratic party prostrate and branded with treason, the Republicans had a dominion over the destinies of the country greater than the Democrats had ever wielded.

Wherever there is such tremendous power, vigilant self-seekers of every kind are sure to congregate. During the years which followed the war, the ranks of the Republican party were permeated with mercenaries of every type—spoilsmen hunting offices, railway promoters seeking land grants and financial aid from the government, manufacturers demanding more discrimination in the tariff legislation, and the great army of hangers-on who attached themselves to these leaders. The integrity of the party was further injured by the "carpet-baggers" in the South, who, in the name of the federal government and the Republican party, plundered the Southern states and heaped upon them an enormous burden of debt.

In these circumstances, the Democratic party began to revive. It had had a long and triumphant history previous to the Civil War; it had great traditions, and numbered on its roll some of the most distinguished men in American history. The population of the country was still principally agricultural and the cotton planters were soon producing as many bales a year as in the "flush times" before the Civil War.

It is not surprising, therefore, that the Democratic party sought to close up its shattered ranks in opposition to Republican rule. In the South, the whites recovered their predominance; in the North and West, farmers protested against the high protective tariffs; here and there throughout the Union discontent with the railway and corporation policy of the Republican party began to appear; and the spoils system which had flourished since Jackson's day stirred to action a small but vigorous minority of "civil service reformers."

As a result, the Democratic party, in 1884, was able to bring together an effective opposition and to elect Grover Cleveland President, with the support of the "mug-wumps" who bolted the Republicans after the nomination of James G. Blaine at their Chicago convention. This Democratic triumph was short-lived, however, for four years later, when Cleveland raised the tariff issue by his celebrated message of 1887, the Republicans were able to elect Benjamin Harrison by a slight majority. Taking advantage of their victory, they forced through the McKinley tariff bill, though it was regarded by many members of the party as entirely too drastic. In the succeeding election of 1892, Cleveland was again able to lead his party to success, but it could scarcely be said that any vital issues now divided the two contending parties.

Chapter VI

Economic Changes and Growth of Dissent

ALTHOUGH the two historic parties commanded the allegiance of the mass of the people during the period just reviewed, there was always a dissenting element in each of them. In fact, every party is a more or less miscellaneous aggregation with a conservative right and a radical left, shading off into each other by imperceptible degrees. If a citizen does not approve the policies adopted by the party with which he is associated by birth or temper, he has three choices before him. He can stay within the party and work to secure the nomination of other men and the declaration of other principles. He can go over to another party which more nearly represents his idea about politics. Or he may leave his party and join others who are of a like mind in forming a new organization. Since the candidates and platforms of the major parties usually represent the middle average, the person of extreme views is likely to be disgruntled with them, especially in times when changing circumstances call for sweeping political adjustments.

And in the closing decades of the nineteenth century an economic advance produced a social transformation more revolutionary in character that that which formed the basis of the Jacksonian upheaval. Small business concerns grew into gigantic corporations capitalized at untold millions and controlling nation-wide industries. In this process were built up colossal fortunes from which the total national debt of Washington's day could have been paid many times over. By 1890, the western lands, once a refuge for the wage laborer of the East, were practically all taken up; and the vast timber and mineral resources of the nation had passed largely into private hands. Cities grew by leaps and bounds, and millions of poor were crowded in congested quarters. The village workshop, the old-fashioned woolen mill by the brookside, the hand-loom, the short railway line, and the small individualistic factory were conquered by mighty captains of industry, whose bold enterprises and remarkable genius for world-wide organization are the wonders of our age.

With this second economic revolution came an immense increase in the number of industrial workers. It may be demonstrated, of course, that there are many gradations of fortune in modern life and that wage earners are constantly passing to other ranks, but the fact remains that a permanent and growing working-class, dependent for a livelihood almost entirely upon the sale of labor power, is the inevitable concomitant of industrial advance.

In connection with commercial enterprises, insular dependencies were acquired and the national government was drawn more closely into the mesh of world politics.

Naturally, the new conditions of American life forced to the front appropriate doctrines. As far as they involved radical changes, these doctrines usually found their first exponents in minor parties; and as the respective issues came within the range of practical politics, they were presented to the country in national campaigns by one or both of the two great parties. Accordingly, it is necessary to review briefly the minor parties since the Civil War, for, in spite of their apparent insignificance, they have been important factors in the American governing process. These parties fall readily into three groups: temperance, labor and agrarian.

§ *The Prohibitionists*

About the middle of the nineteenth century there arose a temperance movement which carried several states for absolute prohibition. A reaction, however, speedily set in, and the temperance question was overshadowed by the great slavery issue. After the Civil War, prohibitionists appeared once more upon the political scene. At a convention held in Columbus, Ohio, in 1872, they nominated a presidential candidate and launched a national party. From year to year they kept up what seemed to be a forlorn and hopeless battle.

At no time did they muster three hundred thousand votes; at no time were they regarded as more than harmless "cranks." But their influence exceeded their numerical strength. Moreover, the idea of prohibition was taken up by leaders in the old parties, who utterly repudiated the harsh and uncompromising tactics of the prohibitionists; and new methods were introduced when the Anti-Saloon League was formed to wage war on the saloon especially by appeals to employers.

In the course of time, hundreds of localities and two-thirds of the states were made "dry" by referendum after referendum; finally the prohibition

of intoxicating liquor as a beverage throughout
the United States was incorporated in the Eighteenth Amendment to the Constitution, put into
effect in January, 1920. Still the question of en-
forcing the Amendment kept the liquor question
"in politics" even more prominently than before
the establishment of legal prohibition. The fortunes of many candidates now depended upon the
degree of their "dryness" or "dampness", but it
could hardly be said that prohibition was a major
issue on which the parties clearly divided.

§ *Labor and Socialism*

Almost immediately after the Civil War, labor
entered American politics as a separate and independent element. In 1872, a party known as the
Labor Reformers held a national convention in
Columbus, Ohio, which was attended by representatives from seventeen different states. At that convention, the party declared in favor of Chinese exclusion, an eight-hour day in government employ-
ments, civil service reform, one term for the President, restricting the sale of public lands to bona
fide homeseekers, the regulation of railway and

telegraph rates, and the subjection of the military to civil authority.

For a time, the labor element seems to have been absorbed into the agrarian groups described below; but in 1888 a Union Labor party met in a national convention at Cincinnati, and drafted a platform embodying the principal doctrines of the Labor Reformers, demanding, in addition, popular election of United States Senators.

Although the American Federation of Labor was organized under its present name about this time, namely in 1886, it lent no countenance to the idea of a separate labor party. Experiments of that kind had been made without marked effect in the days of Jacksonian Democracy, and Samuel Gompers, the president of the Federation, denounced, in season and out, independent political action on the part of trade unions. It is true that the Federation from time to time advocated many specific measures of law, state and national, and gave its support to candidates of the two major parties who declared themselves favorable to its policies. It is true also that the Federation officials endorsed the candidacy of Robert M. La Follette for the presidency in 1924 on an independent progressive ticket, but the small number of votes polled in the election convinced the higher labor officials that the old policy of playing one major party off against the other was a better way of securing influence in politics.

An avowed socialist organization appeared on the national stage in the campaign of 1892, when the Socialist Labor party held its first national convention in New York. This party made its appeal almost exclusively to the working class. It declared that "man cannot exercise his right of life, liberty, and the pursuit of happiness without the ownership of the land and the tools with which to work. Deprived of these, his life, liberty, and fate fall into the hands of the class that owns these essentials for work and production." The appeal of the Socialist Laborites to the working class to unite against the property-owning class met, however, with no considerable response; their candidate in 1896 polled only 36,373 votes; in 1920 the number was about 21,000; in 1924, it was 36,428.

Internal dissensions and the extreme views of the Socialist Labor leaders led to the organization of another radical group, known as the Socialist party, which held its first convention in 1900. At the presidential election of 1908 it polled 448,453 votes—more than the combined vote of the other minor parties. Four years later its vote rose almost to a million, and exerted a decided influence on the two major parties.

This party also made its appeal especially to the working class, but it did not demand the complete abolition of all private property in the means of production. From time to time it declared in favor of graduated inheritance and income taxes; universal suffrage; the initiative and referendum; proportional representation and the right of recall; popular election of judges; employment of idle working men on large government undertakings; collective ownership of all industries in which competition has ceased to exist; extension of the public domain to include mineral resources, forests, and water power; and compulsory government insurance for the working class.

Though fairly united on domestic policy, the Socialist party split on foreign issues. On the one hand, the official opposition of the party to the war against Germany led to the withdrawal of many prominent leaders. On the other hand, the world-wide reverberation of the Russian Revolution forced the remaining directors of the party into a relatively moderate position, producing a conservatism on various matters which brought about a secession of communists in 1919. In the election of the following year, the Socialists polled about 900,000 votes—a figure not equal to that of 1912 if the increase in population and the new votes of women are taken into account. Discouraged by such meager returns and torn by dissensions over Russian principles, the Socialists did not put forward a candidate in 1924 but contented themelves with supporting La Follette, the independent progressive. Extremists on the left wing, the Workers' party, declared in favor of communism, nominated a candidate, and polled about 36,000 votes in that year.

The slight results attained by radicals in their efforts to found a revolutionary party in America by appeals to industrial workers have always been a mystery to European observers. There are trade unions in the United States as in the Old World and there have been many long and bloody struggles between capital and labor on this terrain. And yet revolutionary socialism and communism have made no great headway.

Many reasons may be advanced to explain this. American working people, on the whole, in spite of great areas of poverty, enjoy a standard of life higher than that in Europe. If proof were needed, immigration statistics could supply it. American workingmen have also enjoyed the right to vote for nearly a hundred years, and they got this right without a savage struggle with the bourgeoisie. Finding capitalists and agrarians engaged in a lively battle when they appeared on the political scene and no barriers separating them from the other classes, the majority of workingmen naturally dropped into the party organizations at hand.

All experiments in independent action, such as those made in Jackson's day, ended in failure and convinced even the dissenters that they had more to gain by staying in established channels than by setting up a separate party. Welcomed by the major parties, especially the Democrats, workingmen entered politics freely, obtained elective offices, and climbed to high appointive positions in the government. And this opportunity to obtain power, coupled with the responsibility that went with it, made them cautious about undertaking large reconstructions of society by their own efforts. Nevertheless, the Socialists, who returned to independence in 1928 and nominated as their candidates, Norman Thomas and James Maurer, kept up the fight to develop an independent labor party.

§ *Left-wing Agrarianism*

Not long after the Civil War, a distinctly agrarian party, professing the principles of left-wing Democracy, challenged the right of the major parties to rule. With the rapid decline in the prices of agricultural produce, which accompanied the general collapse of the inflated war prices, the farmers began to grow bitter over their lot and to organize societies, known as Granges. At length they came to believe that the railways, the corporations, and the financial policy of the federal government were principally responsible for the evils under which they labored. Working through the legislatures, especially in Illinois, Iowa, Wisconsin, and other Western states, they attempted to secure relief by means of laws regulating railway rates and warehousing.

In 1876, the discontented farmers entered politics as the Independent National, or "Greenback," party, and waged warfare especially on the Republicans, whom they charged with having brought about the decline in prices by placing the monetary system on a specie basis and contracting the currency. Notwithstanding the small vote polled by their candidate, Peter Cooper, of New

York, the Greenbackers put forward a candidate in the next campaign, and even made a third attempt in 1884. In view of later developments, their platform of 1880 is interesting, for it included, among other things, free coinage of silver, advanced labor legislation, the establishment of a national bureau of labor, Chinese exclusion, a graduated income tax, and the regulation of interstate transportation.

Although it gained in votes at first, the Greenback party went to pieces completely after the campaign of 1884. Within a short time, however, restless agrarians formed a new association, known as the Farmers' Alliance, which, although it did not officially enter politics, was instrumental in creating the Populist party. This party drew together, in 1892, both agrarian and labor elements. At a national convention in Omaha, it put forth a radical program, demanding government ownership of railway, telegraph, and telephone lines, a graduated income tax, postal savings banks, and the free coinage of silver and gold at the legal ratio of 16 to 1.

On this platform the Populists went into the campaign of 1892, and polled more than a million votes, principally in the Western and Southern states, carrying Colorado, Idaho, Kansas, Nevada, and securing one electoral vote in North Dakota and another in Oregon. This unprecedented achievement by a minor party was partially due to fusion with the Democrats in some of the states, but beyond question the Populists had attained a numerical strength which made them a force to be reckoned with in American politics. Indeed, in 1896, the Populistic wing of the Democratic party captured the organization and tested its principles in the memorable campaign of that year.

For a brief period after that exciting contest, the distraction of the Spanish-American War and the prosperity which followed it turned the attention of the country from domestic issues; but the diversion was short lived. Discontent with the tariff of 1909 split the Republican party and merged into the Progressive revolt under the leadership of Roosevelt. In a short time agrarianism appeared again in the Northwest, especially in North Dakota, and though overshadowed by the agitations of the World War, it spread far and wide.

This time the agrarians sought to avoid breaking the sacred ties of party. They called themselves non-partisan. One faction organized the

Non-Partisan League, which worked mainly through the formal organization of the dominant party in the respective states. But the principles of the new faction were almost identical with older agrarian doctrines: stricter regulation of the railways or national ownership, "easier money" for the farmers through state banks and farm loan schemes, state warehouses for grain, agrarian control over the national banking and currency system, and heavier taxes on accumulated fortunes.

Chapter VII

The Upheaval

NOT UNTIL more than thirty years after the triumph of the Republicans in 1860 did the Democrats again make a frontal attack on "the money power" in the style of Jefferson and Jackson, using old and new issues to rally farmers and mechanics to their side of the alignment. Yet slowly through the decades, as we have just seen, a left-wing agrarian movement gathered strength; finally, in 1896, it overwhelmed the Democratic party and split the Republicans.

§ *The Democratic Program of 1896*

Neither in principles nor in language did the Democratic platform of that year depart essentially from the traditions set by the agrarians in the days of Jackson although, of course, new times had brought new devices for conquering the party of "wealth and talents." As of old, the currency question, with all its implications for the distribution of wealth, was a central issue of the battle.

This time, however, the agrarian remedy was not more paper money issued by state banks, but an increase in the volume of the currency to be effected by the free coinage of silver on a ratio of sixteen units to one of gold. The practical purpose was the same, namely, to make it easier for debtors to pay and at the same time raise the price of farm produce.

In dealing with the second historic question, namely, the United States banking system, the Democratic platform of 1896 cited specifically the language of Andrew Jackson and denounced the issuance of notes by national banks as undesirable and unconstitutional. This was true to form.

Equally direct was the plank on protection for American industries: "We hold that tariff duties should be levied for purposes of revenue . . . . and not discriminate between class or section." John C. Calhoun could not have been more explicit.

An income tax was endorsed "to the end that wealth may bear its due proportion of the expenses of the Government." Besides levying on great riches, such a tax would afford revenue to make up for the reduction of protective duties on goods consumed by the masses.

Returning to a tradition temporarily weakened during their long tenure of power in the Middle Period, the Democrats in 1896 assailed the federal judiciary, this time for declaring null and void the income tax law of 1894. Now they spoke of a possible reversal "by the court as it may hereafter be constituted". This was strangely like the language used by Lincoln many years before in criticizing the Dred Scott case.

And what did labor—that other "humble order of society" dear to Andrew Jackson's heart—receive at the hands of the Democracy rampant? A plank denouncing the use of injunctions in industrial disputes and approving "trials by jury in certain cases of contempt."

Having made a platform in harmony with the traditions of the left wing, the Democrats proceeded to nominate William Jennings Bryan, aptly called "the Tiberius Gracchus of the West." There could be no doubt about his position with reference to the century-old battle. In his famous "Crown of Thorns Speech" he had placed himself on the side of the wage earner, the country lawyer, the cross-roads merchant, the farmer, and the miner. He expressly named them as his friends and exclaimed: "It is for these that we speak."

The great question, as he saw it, was: "Upon which side shall the Democratic party fight? Upon the side of the idle holders of idle capital, or upon the side of the struggling masses? . . . . The sympathies of the Democratic party, as described by the platform, are on the side of the struggling masses, who have ever been the foundation of the Democratic party." No line could have been more clearly drawn.

On such principles, Bryan appealed to the country in 1896 and again in 1900, only to go down to defeat before William McKinley, a statesman of the Hamilton-Webster school. Again in 1908, after attempting a conservative tack to the right under Alton B. Parker in 1904, the Democrats swung back to Bryan, adopted a platform even more aggressive in tone, and were vanquished once more at the polls.

§ *The Republican Program*

On their side of the line, the Republicans were loyal to the Hamilton-Webster-Seward heritage. In not a single relation did they depart from the traditions of a hundred years.

In Hamilton's creed, protection for American

industries was a leading article. On coming to power in 1897, the Republicans enacted the Dingley tariff bill which carried the duties, on the average, to a new high level. There were compromises in it, of course, but in the main manufacturers were delighted with it.

Of equal importance in the Hamilton creed were banking and currency. The Whigs and their successors in interest, the Republicans, knew this quite well. Having won a great victory over the easy money party in 1896, Republicans proceeded as fast as circumstances would allow to give attention to that issue. To solidify the currency they enacted the gold standard law of 1900, and, under the leadership of Senator Aldrich of Rhode Island, were preparing to revise the whole banking system, when they were ousted from power once more.

Especially did the Republicans attend to the development of the trading empire which Federalist legislation had favored, Webster had promoted, and Seward had advanced. In McKinley's first administration, they annexed the Hawaiian Islands, waged war on Spain, made Cuba a protectorate, added Porto Rico, Guam, and the Philippines to the American empire, and united with foreign powers in upholding their rights in China. Victorious every time the Democrats assailed them for "imperialism," the Republicans not unnaturally looked upon themselves as commissioned by the people to exploit the resources added to the country by arms and diplomacy.

§ *The Rise of Progressivism*

Underneath the prosperity so vaunted in the age of the full dinner pail, rumblings of discontent on the left wing could be heard as in the days of Daniel Shays, Andrew Jackson, and Andrew Johnson. At no time did the agitations of the populists, socialists, and other dissidents die completely away. Although the makers of unrest, or the spokesmen of it, differed among themselves as to their remedies, they were all united in waging war on what they were fond of calling "government by a plutocracy." With some variations, they demanded an inflation of the currency either by the free coinage of silver or some form of paper, graduated income and inheritance taxes, a reduction of the tariff on goods consumed by the masses, stricter regulation of railways and trusts to cut down their revenues, aid to farmers in the shape of loans at

low rates of interest, and laws designed to improve
the status of industrial workers.

When the prosperity that followed the Spanish
War declined, the agitations of the socialists and
the agrarians became more vigorous than ever.
After the enactment of the tariff law of 1909, the
discontent of Western farmers began to make
marked inroads upon the apparent solidarity of
the Republican party. Indeed, a rift in that party
had been in process since the accession of Theo-
dore Roosevelt to the presidency in 1901, for he
soon aroused the distrust of the capitalistic wing
by appealing to the populistic sentiments cherished in the agrarian wing. In his messages and
speeches, he brought railway, trust, labor, and
other social questions prominently into politics.
He advocated income and inheritance taxes partly
with a view to helping equalize fortunes; he rec-
ommended a stricter federal control of business
corporations; and he advocated a few measures for
the benefit of the working classes.

Discovering that his successor, President Taft,
supported the conservative wing of the Republican
party in Congress, Roosevelt, on the appeal of
many followers, sought the Republican nomination at Chicago in 1912. Failing to secure it,

he and a large portion of his adherents "bolted" and formed a new party, taking the name of "Progressive."

Encouraged by the split in the Republican ranks, the Democrats entered the campaign with great confidence, led by Governor Woodrow Wilson as their candidate. The conservatism of Cleveland and Parker they definitely abandoned.

Now for the first time since its formation, the Republican party was confronted by an overwhelming combination that threatened it in the language of populism. The Progressive platform, on which Roosevelt ran for President, declared that both the old parties had become "tools of corrupt interests" and that "to dissolve the unholy alliance between corrupt business and corrupt politics is the first task of the statesmanship of the day." The Democratic candidate asserted in similar language that "the government of the United States at present is a foster child of the special interests," meaning thereby "the big bankers, the big manufacturers, the big masters of commerce, the heads of railroad corporations and of steamship corporations."

As the Republican party was shattered by the Progressive defection, Wilson was easily elected

President, although his popular vote was more than two millions below the total poll of the opposing candidates.

Within a little more than a year after Wilson's inauguration, the European war broke in upon the peace of the world. American industry and agriculture were made prosperous again by the extraordinary demands of the European belligerents, especially the Entente powers. Social questions which had emerged in 1912 were thrust into the background, and the campaign of 1916, waged while the war was still raging, naturally took on the color of that conflict. The Progressives nominated Roosevelt, only to have him decline. Rejecting Progressive overtures, the Republicans selected as their standard-bearer Justice Charles E. Hughes, former governor of New York; and after Roosevelt refused to accept the nomination, the Progressive national committee indorsed the Republican candidate. In their platform, the Republicans favored maintaining "a straight and honest neutrality between the belligerents in Europe" and the protection of American rights. The Democrats renominated President Wilson and based their appeal mainly on his record of achievement and on the fact that he had kept us out of war.

§ *The Program of the New Freedom*

Although the clangor of the European war made more headlines for the newspapers, as a matter of fact there was enacted during the eight years of President Wilson's administration the most remarkable program of legislation passed since the Civil War. And it is to be noted that this legislation merely expressed in legal letter the spirit of the Democratic platform of 1912.

In the third paragraph, that platform declared that "the high Republican tariff is the principal cause of the unequal distribution of wealth; it is a system of taxation which makes the rich richer and the poor poorer; under its operations the American farmer and laboring man are the chief sufferers." Jacksonian Democracy was never more precise. The platform also condemned the "so-called Aldrich bill or the establishment of a central bank" and advocated "such a systematic revision of our banking laws as will render temporary relief in localities where such relief is needed, with protection from control or domination by what is known as the 'money trust.' " It asserted that "of equal importance with the question of currency reform is the question of rural credits or agricultural finance." The suppression of "gambling in agricultural products by organized exchanges and others" was also promised as a part of a program "to improve the conditions of trade in farm products." Recalling the previous pledges of the party to organized labor, it promised trial by jury in cases of indirect contempt and the relief of trade unions from prosecution as illegal combinations in restraint of trade.

With a fidelity to promises not always observed in American politics, the Democrats under the leadership of President Wilson passed a series of laws that squared fairly well with the historic principles of the Jefferson-Jackson-Bryan heritage.

First of all the tariff was materially reduced in 1913—for the first time since 1857—and in the revision agricultural interests received a consideration which was more than friendly.

Currency and banking questions were attacked in the Federal Reserve Act. As if to recall the tussle of Jackson with an independent corporation, this Act put the control of the new banking system in the hands of a political board appointed entirely by the President and Senate. Bryan had declared that gold was too narrow a basis for the currency: the Federal Reserve Act provided for the issue of money on prime commercial paper— in practical operation going far beyond the gold foundation. Bryan had been accused of demanding a fifty-cent dollar for debtors and farmers: the country lived to see a dollar worth less than fifty cents in the market place. Jacksonian Democracy had feared a centralized "money power": the Federal Reserve Act attempted to distribute that power throughout the whole country by creating twelve separate banking districts.

In keeping with their professions, the Democrats, while framing their revenue program, resorted to the income tax—that old device of the Populists, now made constitutional by the Sixteenth Amendment. To render it quite palatable to the left wing, they placed the exemptions at a good figure and made it progressive, increasing the rates as riches mounted upward. Under the financial stress of the World War, the income tax, individual and corporate, rose to percentages in the higher brackets that fairly staggered the possessors of great fortunes. Besides being besieged to give to war charities "until it hurts," they were compelled to pay taxes until it caused positive anguish of spirit and a serious depletion in purse. Nothing like it had occurred during the Republican administration of the Civil War.

"Big Business," so called—the concentration of "wealth and talents"—was attacked by the Clayton Anti-Trust Act of 1914, designed to break up monopolistic undertakings and force price reductions by competition. In line with this measure was another law creating the Federal Trade Commission and endowing it with power to force the adoption of "fair practices" by business concerns in various relations.

Besides the pleasures and advantages conferred by these laws, such as they were, farmers and planters received aid through the Farm Loan Act which enabled them to keep money in their pockets by borrowing at a lower rate of interest than had been customary, especially in the West and South.

Labor, that powerful ally of Jacksonian Democracy, was not forgotten in the program of the New Freedom. It secured so many lines in the Clayton Anti-Trust Act that Samuel Gompers called the law "The Magna Carta of Labor." It is true that most of the gifts turned to ashes in the fire of judicial interpretation, but labor did not blame the Democratic party for this untoward outcome of its efforts on behalf of the "plain people."

If, as may be surmised, this program of laws did not restore farmers, planters, and mechanics to the position they had enjoyed in the days of Andrew Jackson, it certainly was conceived with reference to their state of mind rather than to the "special interests" so vigorously attacked by Wilson in his presidential campaign. Without question, there would have been a square alignment on this legislation in 1916 if the World War —so profitable to both American business and agriculture—had not intervened and obscured somewhat the ancient political division. If there was any doubt on this point at the time, it must have been cleared in the very first presidential campaign waged after the conclusion of the War.

In the sphere of imperial and foreign affairs, the Democrats certainly made movements in the direction of retrenchment. Their platform of 1900 denounced the "greedy commercialism which dictated the Philippine policy of the Republican administration...and the war of 'criminal aggression' against the Filipinos." "We assert," ran the document, "that no nation can long endure half republic and half empire, and we warn the American people that imperialism abroad will lead quickly and inevitably to despotism at home."

True to their tradition, the Democrats did not oppose expansion, "when it takes in desirable territory which can be erected into states in the Union and whose people are willing and fit to become American citizens." But they were against the imperialism of commerce—absorbing subject races and the development of trade and investment opportunities through military power. Again and again, the Democrats repeated this profession of faith. In 1912, for example, they declared: "We condemn the experiment in imperialism as an inexcusable blunder."

When in a position to give effect to their creed, the Democrats naturally spoke more softly, but they did not overlook their pledges. They gave more self-government to Porto Rico and the Philippines, promising the latter independence sometime in the future. In dealing with the Far East, President Wilson looked coldly upon the devices of "vigorous diplomacy." He at first declined to lend his sanction to projects of international bank-

ers, known as the consortium, for lending money
to China and introducing a certain administrative
control over her finances. He refused to utter
any threats against Japan, even when she made the
"twenty-one demands" upon China and he so
neglected American interests in the latter country
that his own minister at Peking threw up his office
in disgust.

Nearer home, however, especially in the Caribbean, President Wilson continued the strong
policy which had been inaugurated under Republican auspices. It is true, he promised the Latin-
Americans freedom from intervention on behalf
of economic interests in the United States but for
one reason or another was unable to carry out his
pledges.

Nevertheless when he entered the World War,
he condemned imperialism in terms almost savage
and at the Paris peace table he sought no material
advantages for the United States in the distribution of the spoils of victory. Moreover he proposed a League of Nations which seemed to
threaten some kind of international control over
undeveloped races, some limitations on the exploi-
tation of the backward countries by powerful
peoples, and the possible interference of a super-

state with the ordinary processes of imperial expansion. At all events, statesmen of the McKinley school did not believe that Wilsonian doctrines expressed in the League Covenant squared with the traditions which their party had followed since the days of Webster and Seward.

CHAPTER VIII

RESTORATION AND HEALING

"**A**MERICA'S present need is not heroics but healing; not nostrums but normalcy," exclaimed Senator Warren Gamaliel Harding in an address delivered to Boston businessmen in the spring of 1920. In twelve words, the Senator expressed a poignant longing that certainly was widespread. He was himself of the McKinley school and knew very well that for nearly two decades the course of business enterprise had been disturbed, first, by Roosevelt and then by Wilson.

Strictly speaking, both of them could be regarded as "political accidents." Roosevelt had been elevated to the presidency by the assassination of McKinley. Wilson had slipped into that high office during a scrimmage in the Republican camp. All the while the number of people engaged in business enterprise, as distinguished from agriculture, and the amount of capital employed in that branch of economy had been increasing. There was some justification for believing that the clock started by Alexander Hamilton could not be set back.

If Wilson's legislation was directed to farmers, planters, trade unionists, and the lower middle classes, it certainly did not seriously cripple industrial undertakings, perhaps because the demand of the warriors in Europe more than made up for losses in the domestic market. At all events, the World War made several thousand millionaires in the United States, thereby adding strength to the Republican, rather than the Democratic, side of the political alignment.

With fitting propriety, the Republicans nominated as their candidate for President, in 1920, the maker of the captivating slogan, "normalcy." On the other hand the Democrats selected for their standard bearer, James M. Cox, of Ohio, and endorsed the principles and measures of President Wilson, including the proposed League of Nations.

In the campaign which followed, it was made perfectly clear that normalcy meant a return to a high protective tariff, a reduction in income and inheritance taxes, less "government interference with business," vigorous naval and diplomatic support for foreign commerce, and a resort to "firm policies" in the Philippines and the Far East. Against this program, the Democrats offered the record of the Wilson administrations and the League of Nations.

Only with reference to the League of Nations was there any marked division of opinion among the hosts marshalled under the banner of normalcy; and in the end that did not prove to be serious. On the whole, the Republican leaders of practical experience were against the League. They knew that the United States now had a good navy and were convinced that the development of the commercial empire, especially in the Caribbean and the Far East, could be more effectively managed if they were free from formal international scrutiny and control. On the other hand, the Democrats had repeatedly condemned imperialism. President Wilson had denounced it in strong language and frankly offered the League as a kind of remedy for the wars in which commercial rivalry had so often involved the great powers. With the issues fairly joined, the Democrats went down to the most terrible defeat ever suffered in the long history of their party.

Before President Harding had gone very far on the way back to normalcy, death cut short his career, leaving his high office to the Vice President, Calvin Coolidge, of Webster's state, a competent political leader even more determined, if possible, to effect the restoration which his predecessor craved. If for a time he was blocked in his designs by agrarian members of Congress, it was made manifest in due course that he had correctly gauged the temper of the majority. Nominated for the presidency by the Republicans in 1924, Coolidge easily overcame John W. Davis, the Democratic candidate, and Robert M. La Follette, the candidate of independent progressives and socialists. Once more there was a landslide. The Republican vote was far in excess of the combined total polled by the two opposing parties.

Concerning the significance of this triumph there could be no doubt. The philosophy of Coolidge was well known. He had once said emphatically that "the driving force of American progress has been her industries. They have created the wealth that has wrought our national development . . . Without them the great force of agriculture would now be where it was in the eighteenth century." Nor was there any confusion in his concept of the party alignment. He regarded himself as the heir of William McKinley, and McKinley, he said, had taken up "the work of Hamilton and Clay . . . reëstablished their principles."

During the years of Republican administration under Harding and Coolidge, long-standing policies of the party were put into effect:

1. In harmony with the doctrines of Hamilton, Webster, and McKinley, the Republicans raised the protective tariff which the Democrats had reduced under the leadership of Wilson.

2. Although President Wilson had kept the Federal Reserve Bank out of the hands of Bryan agrarians, its administration was not quite to the liking of his successor. Under Harding, the high control was moved over to the right—so far in fact that the left-wing Republicans insisted on having a "dirt farmer" added to the Board in Washington.

3. Roosevelt had given pain to the conservative wing of his party by appointing Oliver Wendell Holmes to the Supreme Court and Wilson had positively scandalized the same group by selecting Louis D. Brandeis for that high tribunal. Though these liberals were somewhat offset by appointments of another kind, their dissenting opinions on occasion were not pleasing to the

normalists. Hence, under the renewed Republican régime, William Howard Taft, whose conservative political views were well known, was elevated to the post of Chief Justice, and other selections were made from the same school. Very soon jurisprudence registered a turn in the direction of Marshall's Federalism.

4. For businessmen eager to develop the natural resources of the country, the Harding administration made the way smooth by a leasing policy none too strict in its terms. In fact, in this connection there occurred certain scandals which recalled the misadventures of the Grant administration some fifty years before.

5. Income, excess profit, and inheritance taxes were materially reduced, particularly with reference to the heaviest burden bearers.

6. Foreign commerce was promoted with all the engines of the federal government, the Secretary of Commerce, Herbert Hoover, taking the active lead in this operation, with the general support of the State and Navy Departments. In 1928, a carefully conceived scheme for subsidizing the merchant marine was embodied in the Jones-White Act.

7. The commercial empire was renewed in

spirit. In the Philippines the strong hand was restored. Firm warnings were issued to Japan, calling attention to American interests in China and indicating that trespasses would not be permitted.

8. As a corollary, perhaps, of foreign and imperial policies, the League of Nations was utterly rejected by the Republican administration and direct support was given to the advance guard of American businessmen wherever engaged on the frontiers of enterprise.

Beyond cavil, the return to normalcy brought with it prosperity to the industrial world. But it had to be admitted that farmers and cotton planters did not find prosperity running over the brim of their cup. On the contrary, they received low prices for their produce, suffered from a heavy burden of debts, and eagerly pressed for relief at the hands of Congress.

As of yore, agrarian discontent appeared in the left wing of the Republican party—the party formed by the union of industrialists and farmers at Chicago in 1860. Indeed, as the Democratic party became more urban in tone and direction, the Republican agricultural group steadily developed in strength. It was a highly significant fact that in 1924, Senator La Follette, essentially a spokesman of agriculture, polled more votes in twelve states than did Davis, the Democratic candidate.

As time passed, three features of the century-old contest between agriculture and capitalism became increasingly evident. First of all, the gravity of the agricultural problem was now dimly appreciated in circles accustomed to crying down the farmers as "crazy populists." Since tenancy was rising, the question was asked by responsible statesmen: "Are American farmers to sink down into a semi-servile condition akin to that of the Roman *coloni?* If so, what bearing does this have on the future of American civilization?" Even manufacturers, alarmed at the development of foreign competition under the direction of American investment bankers, began to take a more serious interest in the fate of their best customers— the farmers.

In the second place, the farmers were no longer content with classical remedies for agrarian distress, such as currency inflation. They now demanded a kind of socialization of their industry, with government assistance, and the fixing of prices by elaborate agencies. Such was the underlying animus of the McNary-Haugen bill vetoed by President Coolidge in 1928. As stanch individualists, farmers could never effect by private arrangement an organization comparable to that brought about among capitalists and fix their prices at dinner conferences. Hence they demanded that the government undertake the task. Moreover, the experiment was to be expensive, not as costly as the additions to the navy made necessary by the commercial empire, but still very costly, entailing perhaps a long continuance of income and inheritance taxes.

In the third place, the agrarian group now had leaders quite different from Bryan of 1896—men like Frank O. Lowden, for example, who besides being capitalists in their own right, stood firmly on the contention that the future of America was really at stake, that the fundamental question of maintaining a balanced economy of manufacturing and farming was actually involved, and that a decision in favor of unfettered capitalism would be ruinous in its consequences. In short, the struggle between capitalism and agriculture, it was said, had come to a turning point and the future of the nation's economy hung in the balance. But in 1928 the Republican and Democratic parties both refused to take the drastic steps demanded by the agrarians; the age of Jackson and Bryan had come to a close.

§ *By Way of Summary*

Reviewing this long political conflict certain conclusions seem to emerge.

Political Federalism of the Hamilton type has practically disappeared. No responsible statesman now speaks of the masses in the fearsome and contemptuous language used by eighteenth century leaders, such, for example, as John Adams and Gouverneur Morris. The idea of giving property a strategic frontier by qualifications on the right to vote and hold office is no longer ardently championed. Political democracy, subject to some limitations, has become accepted. When the opponents of Andrew Jackson rallied the conservative forces of the time, they were careful to speak of themselves in the manner of Jefferson's followers, as Republicans, "National Republicans," not Federalists. By changing later to the title "Whig" they merely indicated that they were resisting "executive tyranny." Again, two decades afterward, when a new combination was formed against the triumphant Democracy, Jefferson's symbolism was once more chosen. Appealing on one hand to farmers and mechanics, the party of Abraham Lincoln made a shrewd play by taking Jefferson's popular title and calling itself "Republican."

Economic Federalism of the Hamilton type—with fundamental consistency, repeating the principal items of faith—has continued steadily to the present time. It was and is primarily the working philosophy of business enterprise. It holds that the wealth, the comfort, and the mechanical, scientific, and commercial advance of America are essentially due to business enterprise and that the policies of government associated with it are necessary to its operations and expansion. In an unbroken line, the economic principles of Hamilton were carried forward by Webster, Lincoln, McKinley, and Coolidge. The only noteworthy departure in appeal during the nineteenth century was the open partnership made with the Western farmers in 1860, which gave the party of Hamilton a strange agrarian tinge, particularly in times of distress in the wheat and corn belt.

On the other side has been the frank alignment of agricultural interests made by Jefferson, continued by Jackson (who added an army of

mechanics), solidified by the slave-owning planters, and marshaled anew by Bryan after division
in the Civil War. In this party also, except when
it swung too violently to the left, were to be found
many importing merchants and other capitalists
(with their professional associates) whose undertakings were injured or at least not benefited by
Federalist-Whig-Republican adventures in political economy. As time went on and the country
became increasingly industrial and urban, the capitalistic wing of the Democratic party acquired a
power fairly proportioned to its economic
strength. The events of 1928 registered the decided
shift in the center of economic gravity within
that party.

To some extent, it is evident from the story, the
long political battle has involved the distribution
of wealth directly. It is true that the party of
Hamilton, Webster, McKinley, and Coolidge
never admitted that it was attempting to divert
goods from the agricultural to the industrial class.
Perhaps, in fact, it has added more to the riches
of the country by the stimulation of production
than it has actually collected from the farmers and
planters in subsidies, bounties, and higher prices
under protective duties. The old slogan, "The

foreigner pays the tariff," may have an element
of truth in it. But the leaders of the Republican
party have more than once asserted that the left-
wing agrarians were "assaulting accumulated
wealth"—bluntly attempting to take goods from
the rich—by currency, banking, and taxing
measures.

The latter, the agrarians, have been equally
sure that the Hamilton-Webster-McKinley-Coolidge wing has been engaged in enriching capitalistic classes at the expense of the masses. They
have often been frank in declaring their purpose
to make a diversion of wealth to their side by
currency, banking, and taxing measures.

Whatever the truth in the case as far as economic substance is concerned, in fact leaders in
both historic parties have believed that their
operations involved a contest over the distribution
of goods, sometimes subtle, sometimes crude, but
always very real in character. In politics it is
beliefs that count. In that great game, opinion
and conflict have evolved together. It is impossible to discover to what extent the one is due
to the other, although we may suspect with the
poet that in the beginning was the deed.

Among the instrumentalities employed by the

two parties in this contest over the distribution of wealth, the tariff, currency, banking, and taxation have been constant factors from the beginning. As time has gone on, however, the conflict has become more complex. Today the agrarian interests have abandoned currency-inflation as a method of farm relief and, like the capitalists, are demanding positive measures of government intervention calculated to raise the prices of their products, that is, to affect the distribution of wealth by political action.

When charged with abandoning the ancient creed promulgated by Jefferson respecting "the less government the better," the agrarians either ignore the indictment or point out the forms of government intervention employed by industrialists to keep up the prices of manufactured goods. Discrimination in this relation is difficult.

If either party to the struggle has ever sacrificed a substantial interest to consistency in political theory, history gives no record. Democrats, in 1850, were willing to make a drastic use of government engines to secure the return of property in runaway slaves. Forty years later Republicans, who had professed a liberal view of the Constitution with respect to the things they favored, vigorously denounced the income tax as a violation of that fundamental law, even though a similar tax had been imposed by a Republican administration to finance its war for the Union. At the opening of the new century, President Coolidge, heir to Federalist traditions, finding Congress inclined to make experiments in social legislation for ends not like those of protective tariffs, made strong speeches on behalf of "state's rights."

Surely no one who has examined the relation of constitutional and political theory to practical ends or observed the use of it by both parties can conclude that it is a determining factor in driving men into one party or the other. Indeed this type of speculation, if examined closely, looks more akin to protective coloration than to causation.

A similar conclusion has been reached by some historians after studying the evolution of theory respecting the judiciary. When the Jeffersonian Republicans were being baffled by the decisions of the Federalist Chief Justice, John Marshall, they were highly critical in their attitude toward the federal judiciary. When the same Supreme Court, under the direction of a Democratic Justice, Roger B. Taney, upheld slavery in two ringing decisions, Jeffersonian Democrats, then led by planters, called for loyalty, and criticism came from the other side of the line. Within forty years the tables were reversed and Democrats were assailing the judiciary for its income tax and labor opinions. Still, on the whole, it must be said that the Hamilton-Webster-McKinley-Coolidge party has maintained a more friendly attitude toward the federal judiciary and has had good reasons for so doing.

Now we come to expansion and commercial empire. Jefferson's agricultural party has been fairly consistent in its attitude toward the acquisition of land—for the use of planters and farmers. There is not much mystery about this. Under the auspices of that party, Louisiana was purchased, Florida acquired, Texas annexed, and an empire wrested from Mexico. In waging war on the imperialism of the McKinley epoch, the Democrats made it clear that they did not object to expansion provided it took in desirable territory and people "willing and fit to become American citizens." On the other side, the Federalists generally opposed western expansion on the ground that it would enable the farming population to overbalance, that is, outvote the commercial sections.

With equal attention to substantial matters, the Federalist - Whig - Republican party supported commercial empire, first by legislation, then by active naval interposition, and finally by war. It was under the auspices of this party that favors and bounties were given to shipping, formal relations with China were begun, Japan was opened, Hawaii acquired, and Porto Rico, Guam, the Philippines, and other territories added to the American heritage. Opposition to such enterprises, such as it was, came mainly from the agrarian party.

In this conflict between agriculture and capitalism, which has been at the heart of the American party battle, is to be found some clue, at least, to the existence of two parties in the United States as distinguished from the multiple party system of Europe. American society has been simpler from the beginning than European society. There have been here no racial minorities with historic roots and special territorial interests, such as once furnished the Polish party for Germany and now supplies the Alsatian party for France.

The army of the United States has been small, for obvious reasons, and has never constituted a great separate class in the American social system. The various churches, while undoubtedly powerful in influence, have never possessed large landed property or high offices in the state. Hence there has been no practical nutriment for clerical and anti-clerical parties. So the conflict between agriculture and capitalism has not been confused by collateral issues. Moreover the size of party machines and the expense of maintaining them work against the rise of small parties in the United States. It is usually easier for a person with a new idea—if it is not too radical—to get a hearing in one of the major parties than to attract a following by pursuing an independent course of action.

§ *Where Are We Going?*

At the end of such speculations one cannot help asking: "To what extent have the political parties controlled the development of the country and to what extent have they merely reflected movements and groupings derived from economic activities of the people?" This is an old question. A similar problem puzzled the Greeks and nobody has ever been able to solve it.

Two or three times in the history of the United States, political decisions, seemingly momentous in consequence, have been made. One was in 1787-88 when the federal Constitution was adopted, giving an immense impetus to business enterprise. Another was in 1800 when the agricultural party was put into power and proceeded to acquire all the land between the Mississippi River and the Pacific. A third was in 1860 when, as a result of the election of Lincoln, the planters were unhorsed and subjugated to businessmen and farmers.

From all this we may conclude that politics is not mere sound and fury, a futile game in which the prime consideration is to get the right man and the right slogan. Certainly from the beginning to the end, economic realities as substantial as capitalism and agriculture have been behind the party battle. It can hardly be denied that the center of gravity in accumulated capital has been on the Hamilton-Webster-McKinley-Coolidge side of the contest, although it has been strongly supported by freehold farmers, North and West, since the formation of the union of hearts at

Chicago in 1860 on the basis of reciprocal concessions. Neither can it be denied that the Jefferson-Jackson-Bryan array was essentially agrarian
in its economic philosophy and practical measures
—with an active mechanic-labor wing after the
upheaval of 1828.

But it is difficult to believe that the election
of Blaine instead of Cleveland in 1884 or Parker
instead of Roosevelt in 1904 would have made
much difference in the economy, social life, or
general culture of the American people. Indeed,
it may be said that, given a vigorous, ingenious
race endowed with marvelous natural resources,
the final triumph of business enterprise was as
inevitable as the movement of the suns. As far as
the great body of social legislation enacted during
the last thirty years is concerned, it must be con-
fessed that it sprang from movements of opinion
quite outside the range of political orthodoxy,
that is, from the agitations of minorities winning
concessions from the major parties.

To some extent, certainly, the conflict between
these two parties has been an emotional antagonism arising from divergent economic situations.
The same violent outbursts of temper have appeared on both sides—the superior education of

the rich making little impression on the verbal patterns employed to express their passions. Yet to some extent also, the party antagonism has been due to a difference of opinion with respect to the values of agriculture and capitalism.

Jefferson certainly had a very clear-cut ideal for the nation — one thoroughly "reasoned" although perhaps the materialist might wish to point out that it was an agriculturalist's praise of agriculture. But it was not a slave owner's concept, and Jefferson was a slave owner. On the contrary, it was a freeholder's ideal. The Republic of which Jefferson dreamed was to be composed principally of freehold farmers owning the soil they tilled. There were to be towns and villages, of course, but they were to be small and their prime function was to supply the wants of farmers. Great cities of capitalists and "mobs" of artisans were to be avoided like poison; factories were to be kept in Europe. A complete system of education from the primary school to the university was to open careers to talent, to furnish abilities for the state, and to promote culture for society. A simple government, inexpensive to operate, owing its authority to popular majorities, was to maintain order and defend the heritage. Peace with all mankind was to be a fixed policy, so that this utopia might be continued indefinitely.

Whether this dream could have been realized if Jefferson's party had labored at the task night and day with all the engines of government in their hands affords an interesting, perhaps a melancholy, subject for speculation. But all members of Jefferson's party did not always labor under the spell of this fixed vision. Neither did Jefferson as a practical politician. Yet to a certain extent it was realized, more on account of the immense area of free land available than on account of the political measures adopted by Democratic administrations.

Nevertheless, it is no longer the dream of the Democratic party with its huge urban membership. In fact, with the growth of the industrial population, the center of gravity in the Democratic party is passing, has already passed from the open country to the cities. The mechanical wing, originally annexed by Jackson, probably outnumbers the freehold section and there are enough capitalists not engaged in protected industries to furnish the sinews of war for a considerable party campaign. For example, from the public utilities operating in cities controlled by the Democrats handsome contributions and inside tips for political managers are available to promote candidacies and party enterprises. Contracts and public works likewise yield magnificent political returns. On the other hand, the power of the cotton planters sinks relatively in the scale. Chained to the Democratic party by their antagonism to the negro, they cannot force concessions by threats of desertion and retaliation.

It is perhaps no exaggeration to say that the Democratic party, founded by Jefferson to represent the agricultural interest, has become the organ of "the mobs of the great cities" which he feared and despised, thus to a large extent the organ of industrial masses of alien origin or immediate alien descent. As the party accustomed to pummelling the people of "wealth and talents," the Democrats also draw to their ranks recruits from the lower middle classes. Indeed, if the statement of the party ideal made by President Wilson in *The New Freedom* is authoritative, utopia is the land which offers abundant opportunity for the poor boy to rise into the heaven of the middle class by building "a small but independent business" of his own.[1]

On the other side of the battle-line, the utopia to be won by political action has never been so perfectly sketched by leading participants. Hamilton's ideal, no doubt, was a society in which the rich and well-born governed without any questions from below, industries flourished, and the poor, though compelled to work, were not unprosperous. During the middle period, Hamilton's spiritual heirs spoke of developing manufacturing to such a point that it would supply an adequate market for farm produce.

McKinley did not go far beyond this concept in choosing the full dinner pail for his symbol. None of the men busily engaged in promoting machine industry seem to have conceived of the day when capitalism would be dominant beyond

---

1. These paragraphs were written in May, 1928. The subsequent nomination of Mr. Hoover, the distinguished engineer and promoter of business enterprise, by the Republicans, calls for no comment. Neither does the nomination of Governor Alfred E. Smith, of New York City, by the Democrats. The agrarian wing in both parties was relegated to the rear. The two platforms, strikingly similar, perhaps foreshadow the day when the United States, with respect to industrial capitalism and finance capitalism, will enter the stage of economic evolution already reached by England. In such a case, labor might swing heavily over to the side of industrial protectionism in the interest of high wages, while the unorganized farmers would continue to sink in the scale of economic and political power. Taking into account borrowed capital, farm earnings returned about 3.4% on the investment in 1927-28. In 1927-28, the average wage per farm family was $717 compared wtih $1,301 per person employed in factories. (United States Daily, August 6, 1928.) American capitalism, like that of old Rome, may be compelled to take over large areas of agriculture to feed the urban populace.

all dispute, when three-fourths or nine-tenths of the people would be dwellers in cities, when the export of manufactured commodities would be deemed vital to our very existence, when the United States would be the first naval power in the world, when the members of the industrial army would outnumber freehold farmers five or six to one.

At all events, few of them took the trouble to work out any kind of ideal goal for machine industry, offering peace and security to labor such as Jefferson conceived for the farmer. The nearest attempt on that side was, perhaps, the Progressive platform of 1912, which indeed summed up all the newer social tendencies of the age. Only Socialists have taken the philosophy of the machine at face value and dreamed of carrying manufacturing economy over into a sort of utopia for the industrial masses.

It is doubtless for this reason that individualists of the Democratic school are wont to speak of Socialists and masters of business enterprise as "allies"—unwitting allies perhaps—in destroying the heritage handed down from the days of Jefferson. But this is all speculation and falls outside the province of history.

[149]

70
71
72

74

76
77

79
81

85

88